Modesto On My Mind

Modesto On My Mind

Columns from *The Modesto Bee*

Dave Cummerow

McHenry Museum Press
Modesto, California

LIBRARY OF CONGRESS CATALOGING-IN-PUBLICATION DATA
Cummerow, Dave.
    Modesto on my mind : a collection of columns published in The
Modesto bee / Dave Cummerow. -- 1st ed.
    1. Modesto (Calif.) -- Social life and customs. 2. Modesto
(Calif.) -- Description and travel. 3. City and town life--California--
Central Valley (Valley) I. Title. F869.M675C86 1995
979.4'57--dc20
                                                        95-34513
                                                           CIP
        ISBN 0-930-34904-0 $24.95 (Hardcover)
        ISBN 0-930-34903-2 $12.95 (Paperback)

Illustrated by Steve Odell
Jacket and book design by Ann Christensen and Steve Odell
Cover photograph by Charles Rogers
Printed by Griffin Printing

Manufactured in the United States of America on acid-free paper
First edition

McHenry Museum Press
P.O. Box 4917
Modesto, California 95352-4917
*Publishing house for the McHenry Museum
& Historical Society of Stanislaus County*

DEDICATION

To the Memory of

DIXIE EMMONS CUMMEROW

My Wife of 46 Years and my most Loyal Reader

Foreword

ALL OF THESE COLUMNS WERE previously published in *The Modesto Bee*. I began writing them on a regular weekly basis in 1977 and continued until my retirement in 1989. In March, 1992, I resumed writing them as a regular Saturday offering on the editorial page and am continuing to do so.

Prior to my retirement, the executive editor of *The Bee*, suggested that I compile a collection of my columns for publication in book form. He said he had checked with the late C.K. McClatchy, who was then editor and president of McClatchy Newspapers, who said the company would be glad to undertake publication. On one of my visits to the Mother Ship in Sacramento, C.K. asked me how I was coming with the book. I said I was thinking of it more in terms of a retirement project. He said fine, whenever I was ready just let them know.

Little did I know that before all these overtures were made, he had already received a letter suggesting such a project from Jeannette Maino, who is both a patron and a matron of the arts in Modesto. She is not only an accomplished writer and poet, but she is also a relentless nag who wheedles and cajoles others who show any affinity for the arts to pursue their muse.

Sadly, two months before I retired, C.K., a man several years my junior, died suddenly of a heart attack while out jogging on a Sunday morning.

Over the years, I had developed a personal relationship with C.K. and a great deal of respect for him as an executive and as an editor. His burdens were heavy, and the buck stopped with him. He bore them with courage and goodwill. He never complained about the demands on his time, he never shrank from a hard decision and he never belabored an unfortunate mistake.

After that, I think I lost interest in the project with no will to pursue what I had considered a simple understanding between me and C.K.

Then along came the McHenry Museum Press, the publishing arm of the McHenry Museum and Historical Society, with a similar proposal for publication to coincide with the City of Modesto's 125th anniversary. And this time I was ready.

In this regard, I wish to thank the Museum Press' Publications Committee with Dena Boer, chairman, and members Marge Brooks, David Jolliff and Betty Schroder. This group helped immensely with the planning and preparation of this book, and their knowledge of the inner workings of publication is invaluable.

Also, I appreciate the fully supportive gestures of Sanders LaMont, the executive editor of *The Bee*, and Larry McSwain, the editor who replaced me on the editorial page, especially for his encouragement in having me resume writing after my retirement.

And, I am fully aware of the persistent efforts of my former colleague and good friend, Gerald Perry, who was a co-conspirator in the Maino plot to get this project off the ground.

I should also like to mention Peter Schrag, editorial page editor of McClatchy Newspapers, who was most supportive of my commentaries and occasionally picked some of them up for publication in *The Sacramento Bee*, as did my counterpart on *The Fresno Bee*, Tom Kirwan.

After compiling this collection, I feel I am also indebted to Douglas Carmody, the city's former director of parking and traffic, for the number of times I relied on him and his administration for material for my offerings over the years.

And, of course, I am indebted to Steve Odell, the former and longtime chief artist of *The Bee*, for his outstanding work in supplying the illustrations and design elements for this book and to his wife, Carol, for her kindness and hospitality.

My appreciation also goes to another former colleague and fast friend of longstanding, Emmett Corrigan, for his warm support and superior knowledge of the intricacies of word processors, and to his wife, Hazel, also a longtime friend, for putting up with both of us.

I am also indebted to my good friend and colleague, Chuck Rogers, who used his considerable photographic skills to produce the cover picture with the expert help of Betty Schroder and Bob Hansen, and to no lesser an authority on English than Evelyn Hanshaw who graciously and meticulously did the proofreading of this collection.

Also my gratitude and admiration go to Ann Christensen for the final cover design and layout of the book and for her patience in presenting all the options.

Finally, I must acknowledge the support and encouragement of my son, David, and daughters, Cathy Wooley and Lynne Kellner. They have been among my most faithful readers, and, while not always uncritical, they have often provided inspiration.

I might also recognize a debt of gratitude to the designers of the Briggsmore overpass, but I'll let the book speak to that.

David J. Cummerow

June 1, 1995

Table of Contents

PART I 1
Limited Access: You Can't Get Here From There

PART II 33
Beyond Briggsmore: Now They're Cloning the Evel Knievel
Overpass at Hatch, Beckwith and, Yes, Even Pelandale

PART III 45
Cancelling Our Postmark: No, We Haven't Moved to Stockton

PART IV 55
Wink Van Ripple: The Old Timer Wakes Up Every 20 Years or So
and Wonders Whatever Happened to Modesto

PART V 85
Folk Tales: How the Flatlanders Survive Under the Sun

PART VI 123
Making Connections: Even in This High-Tech World of
Communications, We Still Get Cut Off

PART VII 147
English Spoken Here: Nurturing the Mother Tongue

Part I — Limited Access: You can't get here from there

Next time you're in town...

THESE PEOPLE WERE COMING DOWN from San Francisco. They hadn't been here before. They had freewayed through Modesto, but never stopped off. They had a reservation at the Sundial. The trick was how to get them in there.

Let's see. Maybe the Kansas Avenue off-ramp? No, that's too complicated. Bad intersection just before the tracks. And then sending them down Ninth to make a left turn through a parking lot over to Needham is apt to be confusing. What's the next off-ramp?

Maze Road. Yes. They could take the Maze turnoff and get on Route 108. That means turning left on L Street to Ninth — but be careful. L Street becomes a one-way street the wrong way at Ninth. So turn right and go one block to K Street. That's one-way the right way. Go all the way to the end. Turn right on Needham, go up to the traffic signal and wait five minutes for the left-turn light. You're almost there. You're on McHenry. Now go four blocks past the next stop light. But don't get there around the noon hour or there won't be a place to park.

How about having them get off the freeway at Briggsmore and then take Orangeburg to McHenry?

Give them a chance to live dangerously. Send them on the Evel Knievel overpass. The quickest way to get on Orangeburg is to come up the freeway off-ramp at 95 mph, sail off the off-ramp above the freeway, clear the International House of Pancakes and touch down next to Jack-In-The-Box. Be sure to hit the brakes and rev up the reverse thrust. That curve coming up is about 90 degrees.

Otherwise, it could be dangerous. You come up to the top of the ramp and stop. It is about a six-way stop, so pick a good open-ing and try to get in the right lane. But not too soon. The lane you really want is reserved for cars coming up the northbound off-ramp. Only they don't want it. They're all trying to go to an inside lane so they can turn left at the light down below after clearing the cars backed up waiting to negotiate a left turn into the northbound on-ramp. Like we told you before, this overpass has more left turns than the road to Utopia.

On second thought, scratch the overpass. These people have

never been here before. It took a long time to get them down here. Don't make it look like you're trying to discourage them. By all means, keep them off of that overpass. Tell them it is reserved for natives and daredevils, and the former are getting restless about becoming the latter.

Actually, we need to make these visitors welcome on their first stopover. Have to play it safe. Take the Kansas off-ramp and pull into Monty's Cookery. Have a cup of coffee and phone. We'll come and get you. But don't get there around noon, etc.

—*December 17, 1977*

Our unbecoming modesty

ONE OF OUR ARTICULATE LETTER-writers penned a disturbing note this week. He said it is high time Modesto did something to put itself on the map. Get a few miles away, he said, and nobody ever heard of Modesto. It's exasperating. Even humiliating.

The letter came from S.R. Jaskunas, a physician who dashes off a note now and then in amazingly legible handwriting. He writes on a variety of subjects — usually quite candidly, sometimes with tongue in cheek and always outside the realm of medical community shop talk. Never once has he ever said anything about M.D.'s — like anybody who thinks Hospital M should be second to Hospital D ought to have his head scanned.

Such being the case, it is all the more astounding that anyone so aware and well informed has not discerned what is really going on in Modesto.

Do you think it is an accident that Modesto enjoys so little recognition beyond its sphere of influence? Ha!

Far from it. It is one of the most deliberate and carefully

planned strategies ever devised, widely participated in by a vast consortium of public and private agencies.

Known to the inner circle as "reverse boosterism," the strategy employs both the "dumb farmer syndrome" and the "hidden treasure technique."

Let us remind you that for years we actively discouraged the idle curiosity of transient travelers by running a railroad down the middle of the highway. The railroad is still there but the highway has been moved, a change that could have put us in grave danger. It was averted only by careful planning.

A system of obscure access routes into the city was cleverly devised in such a way that it could only be divined by natives and a handful of clairvoyants. Any strangers who might accidentally penetrate this outer ring are routed immediately into a secondary defense — a one-way street grid that soon has them caught hopelessly in a web of intersections, thrashing around frantically in search of the quickest way out of town.

And the perimeter defense recently has been fortified by redesigning the Briggsmore Outpost.

This plan obviously required the cooperation of the state's highway department, but that agency's complicity goes much further. Caltrans balked at removing all signs pointing to Modesto, but did agree to delete all references beyond the 30-mile limit. The result is that all roads leading to Modesto beyond that radius point to Tracy or Fresno or Vernalis.

That is only the beginning, Doctor.

Why do you think the Amtrak train does not come down the Southern Pacific into Modesto? Why do you think the station was moved to Riverbank? We'll tell you why. When the train stopped at Empire, passengers looked out the window and saw this city creeping up and wondered what it was, that's why.

4

Do you really think United Airlines wanted to cut back its schedule to two daily flights? Security reasons. Too many new people showing interest — especially those on their way to Los Angeles, asking a lot of darn-fool questions about living conditions and other things that are none of their business.

And those tastefully done Gallo commercials that television takes into living rooms all across the land. Ever notice how fast that little line at the end flashes on and off the screen: Gallo Vineyards, Modesto, California. And it's gone. Almost subliminal. All part of the strategy.

But the master stroke in all this, Doctor, was the postmark. It took a lot of doing, but we finally brought the Postal Service around. Now most of the mail leaving here carries a Stockton postmark.

All in all, things are coming along quite well. Oh, we've had a few close calls. They wanted to put a state college here, but we fought that off. Mark Spitz caused some momentary embarrassment a few years ago, and George Lucas has been something of a problem, but we have pretty well convinced everybody that "American Graffiti" was really about Petaluma — a city which suffers from much greater name recognition.

So where is the payoff in this so-called reverse boosterism? For one thing it drives ambitious vice presidents in charge of relocation absolutely wild.

"Chiselton," the boss says, "how are you coming on that Western plant site?"

"J.B., you would not believe what I have found. A diamond in the rough. A light under a bushel. A little place in California made to order and they don't even know what they're sitting on. Two interconnected railroads, highways all around, an airport that the airlines are abandoning, close to everything of importance in

California, and nobody knows about it. Would you believe, J.B., they don't even have their own postmark?"

"What's the name of this Western paradise?"

"Modesto."

"What's that?"

"Moh-des-toh."

"You're right. Never heard of it. But Chiselton, my boy, I'm proud of you. You really pulled it off this time. Fine piece of work."

"Oh, it was nothing, J.B."

"Come now, Chiselton, don't be — Moh-des-toh. That's a joke, Chiselton."

"It sure is, J.B."

—*September 9, 1978*

Showing real initiative

THOSE BAY AREA BAD PENNIES are back. These are the wise guys who have taken great delight in following Modesto's vicissitudes ever since they "discovered" it and patronizingly adopted it as their favorite valley city.

They have not been wholly dormant, however. It's difficult to understand how they found out about Measure A. Life would be much simpler if they hadn't, for several reasons.

First of all, they know nothing about the background and they don't want to know. All they think they know is that Measure A would require the people's approval of sewers. And that is more than enough.

The biggest mistake would be to tell them that Measure A has to do with growth. That immediately reminds them that all their letters from here arrive with a Stockton postmark, and they would want to know again whether we had finally swallowed Stockton or did Stockton get there first.

Even worse would be to try to explain to them the relationship between sewers and growth. That brings out all the dumb lines about "indoor plumbing" and "rooms with a path" and other trite vulgarities.

Actually, any response is futile. Once they got ahold of the text of Measure A, they had all the material they needed. It was obvious when the conversation started.

"Moh-des-toh has to be the most progressive city in the state," they said. "Bar none." There is no point in answering. You just have to grimace and bear it.

"We have had ballot measures to limit taxes, we have had proposals to control smoking, to end discrimination, to save the rivers, to clean the air, to tame the reactors, to open housing, to close schools, to light streets — but nothing compares with your Measure A.

"Moh-des-toh alone has the imagination, the courage, the strength and now the real initiative to give the sewers back to the people!"

Say nothing. Try to keep from wincing. Above all, don't interrupt. It only spurs them on.

"And high time, too. For too many years the gutter politicians have monopolized the sewers. Moh-des-toh is actually topping Proposition 13. Jarvis let the people put a limit on the amount of their money the politicians could put down the drain. Moh-des-toh would go even farther by putting a stopper on the drain."

There's a limit to how long you can let this kind of thing go on, but once these people get on a subject, it's hard to divert them. Even questions about BART didn't sidetrack them.

"Just one last thing. There is one place where the whole country is missing the boat, and you should give it some serious thought."

Brace yourself. Here it comes again. You can't let it drop. You have to follow up.

"The sales tax — it's the opportunity of a lifetime. And you're going in exactly the wrong direction. The county and the cities are all worried about losing the 1 percent tax when you should be seizing this chance to get rid of it."

Obviously, we are hardly in any position to forego $11 million in revenue.

"Don't you see? You drop this tax, and all of San Joaquin County becomes like a free port."

It's Stanislaus County.

"Whatever — but the point is, people would flock to Moh-des-toh to make big tax-free purchases — automobiles, yachts, airplanes, Marin County people would buy their hot tubs — and people driving through the valley would always make it a point to find Moh-des-toh somehow or other and stock up. Think of the mail-order business you could do — even with a Stockton postmark. The potential is unlimited."

It's no use. They don't understand the interdependence of these things. If Modesto lost its $6 million in sales tax revenue, we certainly wouldn't need any Measure A to stop the sewers.

—*February 3, 1979*

Live and let live

WE WERE ALL JUST SITTING HERE, minding our own air service, when all of a sudden Stockton started picking on us.

Our neighbors to the north began building this big case aimed at showing why Stockton is a better site for a regional airport than Modesto.

They gave us to understand that Stockton is so superior to us in so many ways that we really should be ashamed of ourselves for even mentioning the idea.

We don't even remember ever having seriously suggested the possibility, but that didn't stop the Stockton people from pointing with pride at all the things they have that we don't have. They have 40,000 more people, they have an ocean port, all kinds of railroads and highways, a larger college community and better access to places people like to go when they want to get out of Stockton — like San Francisco and Sacramento.

No quarrel there. They have all those things.

But the thing is, we never remember entering a contest to determine which city would make the better site for a regional airport. Our official position has always been that if the Stockton people really believe they can turn their onion-field airport into French Camp International, more power to them. We would undoubtedly use the service, just as we did in those halcyon days when United, PSA and Hughes Air West flew in there. But that support stops short of a willingness to give up our own guarantee of essential air service, just as we didn't when United was also flying in and out of here.

What hurts most about this unprovoked attack is that we have always considered ourselves to be a good neighbor to Stockton. We send all our mail up there and let them put their postmark on it. We keep some of our best yachts up there. We enroll our students in the University of the Pacific and get good pharmacists in return. We also send some students to Delta College. We patronize some of the fine restaurants, we prize the red onions and we eagerly await the first cutting of the asparagus.

This is all by way of assuring the people of Stockton they have nothing to fear from us. They have only to look at our record of accomplishments to satisfy themselves on this point, particularly when it comes to transportation.

We managed for years to keep Amtrak out in Empire until it was threatening to provide better service. We countered that threat by closing the Empire station and keeping Amtrak at bay out in Riverbank.

We also cooperated with the Caltrans people in the Stockton division to provide limited freeway access to our city and have been quite generous in giving Caltrans full credit for the redesign of the Briggsmore overpass.

If none of these gestures is convincing, take a look at what we're doing now. Just when everybody thought we had given up on getting the Tidewater Southern Railway to move its tracks off of Ninth Street after 75 years or so of trying, we're back at it again.

And this time, with our luck, we might succeed because it is not as important as it was 20 years ago when Ninth Street was Highway 99 and was accommodating 10,000 vehicles a day as well as three or four trains. Maybe the safest thing to do would be just to pave over those rails so we could dig them up in 20 years to serve as the nucleus of a light rail system. Light rail is coming back, you know. San Diego has a system that stretches all the way to the Mexican border, and Sacramento is planning one that would help relieve the traffic on the freeways and thereby provide quicker access to Nevada.

There is virtually no limit to the light rail route possibilities here using the Tidewater tracks as the skeleton. The Ninth Street rails could provide direct access to the new community center and perhaps be extended on out to the Salida Mall, coming back along Briggsmore and McHenry and on back to Ninth Street. Running light rail up the middle of McHenry would add excitement on Friday and Saturday nights.

Not only that, but once the sleeping giant to our north awakens to realize its full potential, we could extend our light rail system to give us fast and direct service to French Camp International Airport.

We would then have a very sophisticated transportation system. We could call it urbane transit.

—February 6, 1982

From there to here

IT IS HARD TO SING THE PRAISES OF A CITY if the city doesn't have a song. A city never becomes truly great until someone comes along to memorialize it and popularize it in words and music.

Where would we be had not Tony Bennett left his heart in San Francisco? Or Frank Sinatra had failed to discover Chicago, Chicago? Or Vic Damone had never whispered Paris in the Spring? Or Glenn Miller hadn't taught us to spell Kalamazoo?

Not to worry. Modesto now has its own song — thanks to the talented team of Ross Wurm and Carla Piper. Words by Wurm and music, fittingly, by Piper.

It hasn't quite caught on yet, but give it time. Just remember, with all the show business talent in Los Angeles, nobody has ever turned out a top 40 tune in its honor. Hooray for Hollywood!

Our song is fittingly entitled "Modesto, My Destination." It thus expresses not only a warm sentiment but a lingering problem.

Just last week reader Jean Turner wrote a letter to *The Bee* expressing exasperation over the way Modesto is deliberately omitted on road signs. Coming from San Francisco, she noted that every destination between and well beyond is duly noted, but not Modesto.

She is absolutely right, of course. It's all part of a great conspiracy along with our postmark, Amtrak and air service. An Amtrak train did manage to find its way into Modesto this week, but SP promised it won't happen again.

And speaking of air service, don't think we aren't making progress in that direction, too.

We almost got into a rut again. Aspen Airlines has been providing reasonably reliable Los Angeles service here for 18 months, and travel agents were even beginning to book passengers as far as a week in advance with confidence.

Now we have been saved again by the Civil Aeronautics Board, which says Aspen has gone far enough. After all, 18 months is a long time when you consider that we have had five changes of air service in the last three years. So, for the sixth change, the CAB wants to give us Inland Empire Airlines.

The CAB, which subsidizes our "essential" air service, says, yes, Inland Empire did underbid Aspen on the subsidy required for the next two years, but the amount of the subsidy is not the sole consideration. Inland is in a better position to provide long-term stable service, the CAB said.

Inland plans to begin improving the service immediately by replacing the 50-passenger planes used by Aspen with 18-passenger planes.

You can't blame Airport Manager R. C. Smith for being a little skeptical of the CAB's assurances. He noted that of the last six carriers brought in here by the board, three of them have gone broke.

All of this tends to keep our travelers guessing. We have a friend in Hawaii who usually makes an annual Christmas holiday visit. She decided to delay her trip until March this time and wanted to know what would be her best approach to flying into Modesto.

Well, March! As the air service flies, that is quite a distance. We're not even sure of next month. Finally we told her that for planning purposes at this point her best bet might be to fly to Denver. All planes seem to go to Denver these days. Maybe because it's so high they don't have to descend as far. Then she could connect with that Frontier Airlines flight and come right in to French Camp International Airport.

So, "Modesto, My Destination" is certainly something to sing about. Only one thing keeps nagging at us. Those opening lines:

> We got one-way streets
> and valley fever
> It's easy on the feet,
> but hard on the liver.

Undoubtedly the poetic license held by Wurm allows him to do that, but it bothers the ear. How about:

> We got one-way streets
> and valley fever
> Still, ah know that ah will
> never ever leave 'er.
> Modesto — my destination.

> —November 27, 1982

Following the signs

WE CAME TO A FORK IN THE ROAD and we knew not which way to turn. That sounds as if it came right out of some old pioneer's diary as he made his way across the country in a wagon train.

Actually, it came from a Bay Area adventurer some years ago

who was braving the winds and grades of the Altamont Pass in a daring and determined effort to find Modesto.

He could find signs pointing to Byron, Banta and Bethany, but nowhere to be found was a marker for Modesto.

This was in the dark interim period after the completion of the Westside Freeway, which came to be known as Interstate 5, and the reluctant decision by Caltrans to make a revolutionary change in its policy, a change that was made despite Adriana Gianturco's dire warning that it would materially aid travelers in finding Modesto.

The problem had its origin in the early stages of the I-5 construction. The first phase completed the Highway 580 link from the Altamont to the extension of Highway 132 into Modesto. At that point there was no way to conceal the fact that anyone taking this highway would would end up in Modesto. There just wasn't any other place to send them. So Caltrans put up a big sign spanning the entrance to this new highway designating it as the route to Modesto. It was even lighted at night. Later, as work progressed on I-5, a sign went up alongside Modesto's indicating this was also the route to Fresno. Still later, after I-5 was completed, the Modesto sign came down and the highway was signed with its final approved designation as the route to Fresno and Los Angeles.

This began the short interim period during which Caltrans was able to restore its policy of hiding Modesto. It didn't last long. There were protests from those who once traveled the route and were trying to find it again. Caltrans would not budge in refusing to make any changes in the big sign over the the entrance to the west side route. But it did agree to a modest concession, which came to be known as the Modesto Compromise. It would erect a little unobtrusive sign alongside the road in advance of the fork saying "Modesto Next Right." The sign would be sure to be seen by most sharp-eyed motorists traveling not over 40 miles an hour in the right-hand lane on a clear day.

The motives of Caltrans were not altogether pure, however.

This was at the time Manteca was being choked with Highway 120 traffic and pressing relentlessly for a bypass. Caltrans figured maybe it could get Manteca to forget the bypass by diverting some of the traffic to the west side even at the expense of its hide-Modesto policy. It didn't work. But Caltrans got even by giving Manteca a bypass that was only a week old before it required major surgery to avoid head-on collisions.

Now Caltrans wants to restore the old policy and remove the "Modesto Next Right" sign, a move which is guaranteed not to make it any easier to find Modesto, but one which will surely introduce more motorists to the thrills of the Highway 120 Manteca bypass.

As matters now stand, there is no agreement on what should be done. The Modesto City Council and the Chamber of Commerce want both routes designated, leaving the choice up to the motorist. That might require one sign with "West Modesto via 132 — Thataway" and another with "North Modesto via 205-120-99 — Thisaway."

Actually, there is probably no longer any reason for Caltrans to pursue its hide-Modesto policy. Just send the drivers right on through. We have adequate means of confusing them once they get here. If they come from the north, we'll put them on the Briggsmore overpass. If the come in from the west, we'll head them into L Street the wrong way.

—May 28, 1983

The Stockton connection

WHEN THE CHINESE EMPERORS BUILT walls around their cities — or even their country, for that matter — they knew what they were doing.

You have to fortify yourself or the barbarians will swoop in and take you over.

Short of building a wall, we have attempted to preserve our territorial integrity, but it's beginning to look like a losing battle. Heaven knows, we've tried long and hard.

When the freeway came through, we used all our influence with Caltrans to protect us from easy access. That meant keeping the off-ramps to a minimum, designing circuitous routes into the city with no railroad underpasses and backing all this up with a readily reversible pattern of one-way streets.

These things helped some, but even then traffic on Highway 99 kept increasing, and people were somehow managing to find us.

The only solution was to get some of that traffic off of 99. Again we turned to Caltrans and again we found the highway people cooperative. They rushed to finish work on the west side freeway and then completed the I-5 link to form an effective bypass. Traffic could now move north and south without coming anywhere near us.

At one time, Caltrans wanted to give us a convenient connection to this route by turning Kansas Avenue into a freeway. It took some doing, but we finally succeeded in getting that plan scrapped.

It's hard to say too much for Caltrans. Even after all of these diversionary efforts, they willingly redesigned the Briggsmore overpass to catch the strays that come straggling down 99 from the north.

And they have been most cooperative about signs pointing the way to Modesto. They have kept them to an absolute minimum and, in some cases, even allowed them to remain ambiguous. We couldn't ask for more.

The advent of Amtrak through the valley was another challenge. In the beginning there was a fear that passenger trains would be coming right through the middle of downtown again. With the help of the friendly Southern Pacific, however, we managed to get the trains shunted elsewhere. Empire seemed far enough away at first, but when that began to get a little too convenient, we were able to put them out in Riverbank.

Likewise, we have had no big problem with air service ever since United decided to let us alone. Deregulation has helped a great deal by making it simple to change the airlines serving us every two weeks or so.

At one time we figured our master stroke was the postmark. Having all our outgoing mail postmarked from Stockton has helped tremendously in keeping a low profile.

Lately, however, we have begun to wonder whether we have really been in control all this time. There are now disturbing signs of a long and relentless underground plot to take us over.

Just look back and ask yourself a few questions. Was it really characteristic of Caltrans to be so helpful, to do our bidding in every instance? Where is the district headquarters of Caltrans located? Stockton, that's where.

The same question arises with respect to the postmark. Who handles all our mail now? Stockton, that's who.

Even Amtrak. Which city wouldn't have been served if the trains had used the SP tracks? Stockton, that's which.

Now they are trying to turn French Camp International into our airport. They even were so bold as to rename it the Stockton-Modesto Regional Airport for a few days until our mayor threatened to sue them. They have taken another tack now and are confident the day will come.

With the airport, they will have our planes, our trains, our highways and our postmark.

What's the next step? Annexation?

We may need that wall after all.

—September 29, 1984

The La Loma affair

ONE OF THE RELATIVELY FEW STREETS in Modesto that goes anywhere is also a problem that won't go away. La Loma Avenue. Beautiful La Loma. Pulling onto it from Yosemite Boulevard is almost like entering a private preserve. Arching Modesto ash trees shelter it invitingly against the valley's hot summers, their leaves turning a soft yellow to become a crown of fiery gold under autumn's gentler sun.

The street curves gracefully past Miller Avenue to the traffic light at Wilson School, then continues on past well-kept lawns and flowered borders, dipping down to Dry Creek bridge at Kewin Park and on past Morton Boulevard. Then it climbs quickly back to the reality of a pretzel parkway at the cluttered junction of Burney and Scenic and H and 19th and who knows what else comes in there.

But for that one mile or so, it's a pleasant, restful trip, one that always impresses visitor.

The trouble is that it is also a heavily traveled shortcut, perhaps the most convenient of only three links between the central part of the city and the eastern industrial section.

For several years now residents of the La Loma neighborhood have been trying to get the city to do something about the increasingly heavy traffic. The city estimates that La Loma now handles 19,200 cars a day.

Over the years there has been almost a steady stream of complaints, petitions, save-our-street organizations and other expressions of exasperation.

For a while the city was able to reduce, but not silence, the outcry by dangling the Jennie-Grand bridge in front of the unhappy La Lomans.

The proposed new bridge would turn Yosemite Boulevard into

18

a faster, easier link between the two sections of the city, siphoning off much of the traffic on La Loma. Or so the theory goes.

The La Loma people have never been too sure of that, and now they're tired of waiting. The Jennie-Grand project has been on-again and off-again for years. Now it is scheduled for completion by the end of 1988. Residents want action now. Some of them even want the street closed.

The latter possibility brought a call from a concerned citizen. She demanded to know what "they" are going to do about La Loma Avenue.

We told her they were going to do the same thing they always do whenever they don't know what to do. They're going to study it.

She persisted. That doesn't mean they're going to close it, does it? That, we told her, is one possibility they say they are entertaining. They better not, she said. She goes to and from Modesto Junior College on La Loma and she served notice that she is not about to get into all the Scenic traffic via El Vista or drive all the way downtown on that bottle-necked Yosemite route. Besides, it's a pretty street. Do we really think they might close it?

No. If closing a street because it is too heavily traveled were a solution to our traffic problems, we would have closed McHenry and Scenic and Orangeburg and others a long time ago. The only time that can work is when a better alternative is provided. That is the heart of the La Loma problem. A better alternative is not readily provided because there are only three ways to get across Dry Creek short of fording it — unless you count the Gomes bridge out on Claus.

So, they will have another workshop session next month and maybe some more after that. Then they will spend $10,000 to $15,000 for the study and that will bring us close to the summer.

At that point they will be presented with several alternatives, one of which may well include closing the street. But it will be obvious that as a possible solution, it would be worse than the problem.

It is just one more of the intractable problems faced by the city's veteran director of parking and traffic, Douglas Carmody.

There is one possibility we have not heard mentioned, but it is one that surely must have occurred to Carmody.

Make it a one-way street.

—February 16, 1985

Here they come

SOMEHOW OR OTHER, they found us. We did what we could. We kept the highway signs pointing to Manteca and Vernalis. We moved the train station out to Riverbank. We kept changing the airlines and even pretended we might move the airport to French Camp International. We cut back on bus schedules and moved one bus depot into a relocatable building.

But still they found us. These are the Bay Area commuters we're talking about. They're coming over the hills in increasing numbers and settling here.

There's nothing we can do. The Border Patrol says they have every right to go wherever they want to. And besides, the patrol has its hands full right now with lottery winners.

The people who keep their eyes on these things say the Bay Area commuters are making their way in here, buying homes, renting apartments and purchasing new cars. The commuters use a lot of cars and they find it's cheaper to buy new cars than used cars. When you buy a car you buy two things. You buy the car and you buy the money to pay for it. They find they can buy the money for a new car cheaper than for a used car.

The Modesto Irrigation District, which has to turn on the lights for these people, says new accounts increased by 35 percent in the last quarter due mainly to the influx of commuters.

The invasion has been coming on for some time now. It began in San Francisco when the price of property and rents started going out of sight. People began moving out, looking for cheaper places to buy or rent.

Eventually the prices got too high even for the business and commercial people. When they needed more room, they decided to get out too, and began putting up big new office buildings in places closer to us, like the Livermore Valley and Contra Costa County. Naturally, prices for property in those areas also began to climb.

There are signs that some of the beneficiaries of this flight from the city are not all happy about it. Walnut Creek, which has been experiencing a boom in the development of office buildings, is an example. Voters there approved an initiative measure which requires traffic congestion to be eased before new development can be undertaken. Two new council members also were elected on a slow-growth platform.

Also, in nearby Pleasant Hill, where the office boom is due to hit next, one council member was unseated by a slow-growth challenger.

On the other hand, in Livermore, which was the pioneer in imposing an annual growth limit, two council defenders of that policy lost out to challengers who favor easing the limit.

Whatever happens over there across the mountains, we are certain to feel the effects of it, whether in the form of creeping development or more and more commuters.

For this reason, we feel it is only fitting that we welcome our new residents with a few suggestion for making their lives easier here.

First off, beware of the Briggsmore overpass. Use it sparingly only during off-peak hours and never try to direct visitors in the use of it. They are apt to wind up in Fresno or the Turlock Sportsmen's Club.

Next, watch out for trains on Ninth Street. And bear with us. The city has been working on this problem since 1910 and is hoping to have it solved by the end of the century. Working on the railroad is no easy chore, especially when the railroads keep merging with each other.

Also, stay off of McHenry Avenue, if at all possible. Freeway travelers are not accustomed to McHenry traffic patterns, particularly the suicide lane, which puts drivers who insist on making a left turn on a collision course.

And remember the name of your county. It's Stanislaus. If you want to sound like a native, don't pronounce the final "s". Say Stanislaw.

Finally, for additional helpful hints from time to time, watch this space.

—November 9, 1985

Growing pains

ON THE DAY THE SENATE OVERRODE the president's veto of the highway bill, there was a predictable amount of jubilation around here.

The reason was that the bill contains $13 million to get the trains off of Ninth Street. That's something we've been trying to do off and on for well over half a century.

22

Much of the credit for the legislative achievement goes to Rep. Tony Coelho, who got the money in the bill and kept it there. In the joy of the moment city officials said that when this great event comes to pass there will be dancing in the street — a big party and Coelho will be the honored guest.

All very fitting. And we're sure the congressman understands that this is an open and standing invitation. We can only ask him to have patience and keep his schedule open for the rest of this century. These things take time.

Our parking and traffic director, Doug Carmody, who has the experience to know what he's talking about in these matters, says he would be quite surprised if the project is finished in five years and not surprised if it takes 10 years. Which means it could even take 15 years. And there we are, into the next century.

One of the major stumbling blocks from the very beginning is getting the railroads together. We have to get Southern Pacific to agree to let Union Pacific reroute their Tidewater-Southern trains along a stretch of SP tracks through the city.

The problem is that Southern Pacific isn't keen on talking because they're not quite sure who is running the railroad at this point. They thought they had merged with Santa Fe until the Interstate Commerce Commission surprised everybody and nixed the merger. The railroads are not done trying, but it will take at least until the end of the year before they get another crack at it.

And we all know that even when the friendly Southern Pacific was in charge of itself, it wasn't always easy to deal with. Furthermore, anyone who has made the Amtrak run from here to the Bay Area knows that switching a train from one railroad to another is a tricky business. In going from the Santa Fe tracks to the SP tracks at Port Chicago, the Amtrak train has to start and stop five times, taking anywhere from 15 to 30 minutes. We don't complain because this is all in the interest of safety. Take all the time you need.

In the meantime, we wonder what it will be like around here when the trains finally go.

We got some inkling from the participants in a growth discussion panel this week at Stanislaus State University.

One speaker said we can be anything we want to be. We now have all the planning tools we need to shape our own future; all we have to do is use them carefully and skillfully.

The only problem with that is that now we aren't exactly sure what we want to be. Mainly because we really aren't us anymore.

Ripon Mayor Ed Feichtemeir touched on this point when he laid his city's concern before the panel.

With a current population of 6,500, Ripon has doubled in size since 1980, with about half of that increase from people who continue to work in the San Jose-Santa Clara Valley area.

The mayor complained that these people can't be integrated into the community. They're there because that's where they could find affordable housing.

Well, we're getting an influx of over-the-mountain commuters, too, and it isn't that these people might not like to get interested in community activities. But anyone who spends anywhere from two to four hours a day just going to and from work has little time — or energy — left at the end of the day for doing anything except getting ready to go to work the next day.

So they probably really don't care much about the tracks on Ninth Street or the traffic on McHenry or the Briggsmore expressway.

Just keep the taxes down, the highways open and the weekends pleasant.

By the time the trains come off of Ninth Street, we're liable to be one long bedroom community stretching from Manteca to Greater Ceres. At least.

We could call it the Stan Joaquin Folly.

—April 18, 1987

The joys of growth

IT'S STILL SOMETHING OF A JOLT TO SEE those highway signs. There aren't many before you get here, but once you find your way, the number is startling for anybody who has lived here a few years: Population 172,000

That should scare off most people, but it seems to work the other way. Look at all the trees, they say. A nice place to live.

Well, it was — and still is, although you'll have to pardon those of us who worry about getting too big for our britches. We hate to think the only way we're going to get our postmark back is to develop everything between here and Stockton.

When we arrived, the population was about 35,000. Downtown was busy. The kids were dragging 10th and 11th streets and there was parking on both sides of McHenry.

We got a look at the future when they developed McHenry Village among the vineyards and orchards beyond Orangeburg Avenue.

There was a Joseph Magnin's for the women, Dunlap's department store, W.T. Grant variety store, a big Lucky market on the corner, and it wasn't too long before some downtown merchants began to defect, moving out McHenry way.

It was pretty congested downtown with all the people working and shopping there. Parking was at a premium and meters were on the streets. The Village people made of point of their vast parking space and no meters.

At Christmas, however, it began to get a little congested at the Village, getting in and out from McHenry.

At the rush hour they even had a policeman in the middle of the street with a semaphore. Might not be a bad idea now, if they could find a policeman brave enough to stand in the middle of McHenry.

We had just opened our second high school and named it for Thomas Downey, a respected community educator. Then came Grace Davis High School, named after a beloved teacher who lived to see her monument and sometimes enlivened graduation ceremonies with the wit and wisdom that had delighted her students.

After that came Beyer High School, named after Fred C. Beyer, an outstanding superintendent of schools, whose life was cut short by a plane crash which also took the life of the man he was very likely grooming as his successor, the warm and personable Joseph Howard.

Soon we will have our fifth high school, named after Peter Johansen, former mayor who lives to enjoy the appreciation of his fellow townsmen for his efforts for education.

The only hospitals we had then were Stanislaus County Hospital, out on Scenic Drive where it still is, and City Hospital, a good but small facility operated by the Seventh-day Adventists.

So a group of citizens formed Memorial Hospital Association as a non-profit group and built Memorial Hospital in Ceres.

The Modesto medical community welcomed the addition of hospital facilities but not the trip over the river.

So some Modesto physicians got together, acquired some property on West Orangeburg Avenue and built Doctors Hospital. At first Doctors was small, like a medium-sized motel, and seemed to fit in with the residential neighborhood. Even the residence of a physician and his wife near the corner of Orangeburg and Florida was preserved for many years.

In the meantime, Memorial Hospital, feeling the competition from Doctors, acquired a large site way out in the country at Briggsmore and Coffee Road and developed Memorial North.

While all this was going on, Stanislaus County Hospital, which at one time provided the only 24-hour emergency medical service, changed its name to Scenic General Hospital.

That didn't last long. Eventually, hospitals began to see that emergency service was not only vital but profitable. So all of them began gearing up for it.

The result is that Memorial has been sprawling all over the acreage it acquired. Like an airport, it is never finished. Doctors doesn't have as much space, so it's going to put up a multistory parking facility.

The county doesn't have the money to expand. It just changed its name to Stanislaus County Medical Center.

So, we're back to Square One. We don't have enough hospitals. They're all medical centers.

—July 4, 1992

Tracking our progress

OUR FRIENDS FROM THE BAY AREA were down for a visit, and we have to say they have mellowed quite a bit. They're no longer quite so smug and condescending, not wisecracking about the lack of signs pointing to Modesto or saying all roads lead to Vernalis.

Actually, they have very little trouble finding Modesto anymore, probably because so much of the afternoon traffic seems headed straight for here, and all they have to do is follow.

They still have not mastered the Briggsmore overpass. We tell them that's nothing to be ashamed of. Nobody has. Even those of us who grew up with it find ourselves in the wrong lane and headed for Sacramento when we just wanted to get to Sisk Road.

Bear with us, we tell them. We're working on some overpasses designed to deliver people into the heart of the city.

They want to hear about that. So we tell them about the Kansas Avenue overpass that will take us off Highway 99 or 132, lift us over the Southern Pacific and plop us down right on Needham Avenue.

Sounds great, they say. When?

Well, we tell them, it's tied into the project to get the trains off of Ninth Street. A touch of smugness returns, an exchange of sly looks and a snicker is heard. Yes, they say, you still have those freight trains in the middle of the street getting longer and more frequent.

Possibly, but we're working on it. Our former director of parking and traffic, Doug Carmody, retired to devote the rest of his life to this project. And it may take that long.

He says we are getting there — slowly but surely.

Carmody says getting the trains off Nine Street involves track consolidation among competing railroads — in this case, SP, Union Pacific and Modesto & Empire Traction Co.

No negotiations are more difficult or take more time than getting three long-time competitors to agree on anything — particularly when there is no governmental agency, city state or federal, that can force them into consolidation. That's why so few such plans have been successful.

Even after 11 years of trying, Carmody is optimistic.

Our friends said they hope they will live to see it and so do we. They were really impressed with the restoration of the old SP depot for a transportation center. But they couldn't help but remark about all this great effort to revive a railroad station that never sees a passenger train. Where's Amtrak?

Well, it's still out in the country on the Santa Fe tracks. At one time we were determined to bring it in here on the SP. But that meant even more complicated negotiations on track consolidation and we didn't want that to impede the agreement for getting the trains off Ninth Street. So now we're thinking about building an Amtrak station along the Santa Fe at the eastern edge of Modesto.

Riverbank has long been the station for Modesto passengers, and they are in no mood to give it up. They tried to raise money to build a new station but the voters turned them down. Nevertheless, Riverbank is determined to keep the Amtrak station.

Our friends thought there should be a governmental agency to make that decision.

There is. And it's having great difficulty. Next to the railroads it must be the most reluctant negotiator in the business. It is the same agency that brought us the Briggsmore overpass and the Manteca bypass:

Caltrans.

—*April 2, 1994*

Looking good

OUR FRIENDS FROM THE BAY AREA arrived for another of their periodic adventures in the hinterlands, and again there were no condescending remarks about "inferior California."

In fact, they were absolutely complimentary.

They had no trouble finding Modesto, they negotiated the Briggsmore overpass without incident and made it straight to our

29

house in record time, pleased with the helpful new left-turn lights.

We weren't prepared for such a sudden change, but decided to imply it was about time they woke up and smelled the coffee houses.

They knew great things had been happening when they reached Stoddard Avenue down by the junior college.

Instead of the tooth-rattling ride toward McHenry Avenue, they found a smooth street, its center line handsomely marked with yellow buttons and dotted with reflector lights. The washboard is gone! And good riddance.

Sycamore, too, which they always regarded as one of our most beautiful streets, is clean and sharp with a new surface and fresh markings. They saw it on the right day, just after the city collected the tree trimmings and well before garbage collection day when the toters and curbside materials stand like shoddy sentinels.

Their most extravagant praise was for H Street. Finally, they said, you have a street that befits its buildings. You have the Methodist Church, the Library, the Bee, the Courthouse, the county administrative office, City Hall and now that tall office structure at the corner of H and 10th Streets. When did that happen. Barely finished. Better be careful, they said, with that building and the Red Lion, Modesto is going to get a skyline.

We tried to conceal our pride. It's only the beginning, we said, and immediately wished we hadn't. They wanted to know what was in store.

Well, we said, there are tentative plans to redevelop that entire square block across from the Centre Plaza between 10th and 11th streets.

You mean, they asked, that the old Hughson and Covell Hotels are coming down? We're not quite sure yet. We aren't that far along. What would be going in there? We're not quite sure about that

30

either. Probably a new central office for the schools and possibly a new city hall.

A new city hall? The old one is in pretty good shape. True, but we need more space and, more than that, we could put the police department, which badly needs more space, in the present City Hall.

Not bad, they said. When is all this going to take place? Takes time, we answered, but don't hold your breath. We still have a long way to go.

Your new transportation center took a long time, too, but we'd say it was well worth waiting for. It has greatly improved that area of the downtown, in appearance and very likely in convenience.

Now if only you could get some trains to come in there. Yes, well, we have other irons in the fire.

Speaking of trains, they said, do you still have freights running down Ninth Street. We do.

Talk about a long time, that's been a long time. True, but it's coming. Negotiating with railroads is sort of like peace talks in the Middle East. They move ahead a fraction of an inch.

What about the Kansas Avenue overpass at Needham Street? That's tied to getting the trains off Ninth. Can't start work on that until the trains are switched.

And the Briggsmore overpass? Any chance of improving that? Not really. In fact, we're now concentrating on keeping the Beckwith and Hatch overcrossings from becoming clones of Briggsmore.

Well, you're moving ahead, anyway, and it's good to see that it's happening in at least one city in California.

Thank you, we said quietly.

But don't tell anybody.

—October 22, 1994

Part II — Beyond Briggsmore: Now they're cloning the Evel Knievel overpass at Hatch, Beckwith and, yes, even Pelandale

Underjoyed at overpass

WELL, THEY DID IT TO US AGAIN, FOLKS. The old, inadequate Prescott interchange has been replaced by the new, inadequate Briggsmore overpass.

As a matter of fact, it takes a little thought to decide whether we were better off under the old inadequate than we are under the new inadequate.

Weighing most heavily in favor of the new structure is the fact that it bridges the railroad and discontinues the treacherous Blue Gum Avenue grade crossing. It also provides much improved access to Modesto Junior College West and conveniently links Carpenter Road with the Briggsmore, Orangeburg, Sisk, Prescott, Evergreen maze, provided you remember the sluggish traffic light at the bottom.

But if you are going anywhere else, folks, watch out.

As a crosstown outer link, then, the overpass gets a plus. As an access and exit adjunct to the freeway it is a total flop, probably even dangerous.

To begin with, it features more left turns than the road to Utopia.

If you are coming up Carpenter to head north on the freeway, turn left.

If you are coming out Briggsmore to go south on the freeway, turn left to get on the overpass, then left again to get on the freeway.

If you are coming off the freeway south and headed for Briggsmore, join all of us at the top of the overpass and turn left. Or, if you are headed for Ninth Street, turn right and quickly bull your way across two lanes of merging traffic to get into the left turn lane. But be careful or you will wind up going south on the freeway again.

The Ninth Street access to the freeway north requires much the same sort of needle-threading on top of the overpass. This one is particularly hard to take because before all the improvements, the Ninth Street access and exit from the freeway were relatively simple and direct.

It is painfully obvious that the Briggsmore overpass was conceived in a period of lowered expectations, designed with a vengeance for complainers and built with the austerity of a tight-belted highway budget.

All of which only reminds us of what we went through to get all of these "improvements." The Prescott overpass was inadequate from the day it opened. We grumbled a little about that but suffered it until eventually the state said it would consider redoing Prescott when the freeway was extended between here and Salida.

Fine. Then the money started to run out and the state said the project, which also included the Beckwith Road overpass, would be a little late, folks.

About this time developer Ernest Hahn got into the act. He was counting on that freeway, particularly the Beckwith overpass, by the time his Salida Vintage Faire shopping center was ready to open. So he wanted to know if maybe a million dollars would help speed things along a little.

The state said yes, by golly, provided the city or the county would accept the money and add it on to their share of the cost.

The city quickly obliged with the reasoning that it was the quickest way to get a new Prescott overpass.

Okay. So now we have it. And, for the time being, all we can hope is that Mr. Hahn gets more for his million bucks than we did.

—January 8, 1977

All the traffic we'll bear

THESE FRIENDS FROM THE BAY AREA who think they discovered Modesto wanted to try again. These are the ones who finally decided to stop off here but never could find a freeway off-ramp that took them anywhere. They kept running into parking lots and wrong-way one-way streets.

Like most big-city slickers, they were pretty provincial about all this. They thought it was very funny that anybody could get lost in Modesto or that so many streets ended up on a canal bank.

"Modesto is a nice place to live," one of the wise-acres said, "but I wouldn't want to visit there."

Very funny. But it wasn't too long before they were ready to renew the adventure. And they wanted a new set of directions.

On the previous occasion, we had finally concluded that the simplest way was to take the Kansas Avenue off-ramp, pull into Monty's, have a cup of coffee and phone. Then we'd either come and get them or talk them in the rest of the way.

They thought that was not only quaint but too much trouble.

"How about if we take Briggsmore . . ."

Briggsmore! Whatever you do, don't take Briggsmore. You may never be heard from again.

"Oh, yeah. That's the one you call the Evel Knievel overpass," they said with amused recognition.

We've changed that. It's now known as Hahn's Revenge. But whatever you do, steer clear of it. And for heaven's sake, don't get here during the rush period.

"The what?"

The rush (bite my tongue, never should have mentioned it) period.

"Oh, commuter time, eh? (nasty chuckle). "Hey, fellas, we gotta be careful not to get tied up in Modesto's rush-minute traffic. (Followed by gales of laughter from the other end.)

Very funny.

The challenge was too much. Not only were they determined to take Briggsmore, they came in at 5 p.m. and were halfway up the on ramp by 5:15.

"I couldn't believe it," the driver said. "There were cars all over that bridge, backed up as far as we could see. They'd move one length and stop, move another length and stop. We were doing the same thing. But cars were streaming in off the highway behind us and the ramp was almost full. Made me kind of homesick. Reminded me of the Bayshore when the Giants are at Candlestick and John Denver's in the Cow Palace.

"We couldn't figure out what the problem was until we got to the top. You know what it was? Four-way stops! Honest. They got four-way stops all over that bridge. This lane stops, then one from that lane goes forward; then that lane stops and one car makes a left turn; then — and cars trying to get on and off that bridge from all directions. It took us 20 minutes to get through that maze, and then we almost got sideswiped trying to get into the right lane. That's like thread-the-needle, Russian roulette and Destruction Derby all in one.

"Four-way stops! And all the time we thought there must have been an accident up there."

There was. The whole overpass is an accident. And not very funny.

—May 27, 1978

Thank you, Caltrans

GOVERNMENT ALSO WORKS IN MYSTERIOUS ways. For all these years we've been trying to get government to return our postmark and what happens? They've decided to give us the Briggsmore overpass instead.

That involves two different branches, to be sure, but when you get right down to it, government is government. Not only do the Caltrans people want to give us the Briggsmore overpass, they're

37

going to give it to us. They are letting us have it, you might say.

We should make a counter-offer. They can keep Briggsmore until the end of the century if they give us the Jennie-Grand bridge before then. And if that's not fair enough, they could also arrange to give us the Richland bridge and the Brighton bridge. We're willing to deal.

The hard truth is, however, that Caltrans is going to insist on giving Briggsmore to us, since we have always been a favorite of theirs, and we better begin to think about what we're going to do with it. There are several possibilities:

—We could move it intact to Stockton to be incorporated into that city's crosstown freeway. It would be a fitting act of reciprocity for Stockton's generosity in opening French Camp International Airport to our frequent flyers, and it would put the overpass closer to our postmark.

—We might try the La Loma solution — allowing only one car at a time on the bridge during peak periods. Certainly, we have plenty of traffic lights to work with, and it might help business in Ripon.

—We could consider going back to the old Prescott interchange and prevailing upon the Santa Pacific-Southern Fe to reroute train traffic now that they have so many choices.

—The City Council might want to make a trip to Florence, Italy, to take a look at the Ponte Vecchio with a view of putting in stalls and concessions along the overpass in the manner of the old Florentine bridge across the Arno River. We could accommodate the Farmers Market there on Thursdays and Saturdays and schedule a Picnic on the Overpass for July 4th, assuming that the neighbors will not object.

—And, finally, there is always the divestiture option. We could turn the whole thing over to private enterprise with the challenge to make something out of it. An amusement park, a tollway, a scenic drive, a permanent movie set for Henry Weinhard beer commercials.

There are a couple of other things we also have to consider. One is that Caltrans is not surrendering unconditionally. They are giving us the overpass but not the supporting structure. We get the top and they get the bottom. That means the thing could fall down, and there's nothing we could do about it — although that possibility does present another option.

It also means that we have to take over the upkeep of the roadway. That involves a number of things. Keeping those crash barrels filled with sand or water or whatever they're full of. Making sure the traffic lights are operating properly so that nobody can get through without being stopped at least twice. Maintaining the archipelago of traffic islands and keeping all the signs and lines freshly painted.

The other possibility is even scarier. There is some talk of cloning the overpass on Woodland Avenue. That's all we need.

Son of Briggsmore.

—May 24, 1986

Making the tour

WHEN PEOPLE COME TO VISIT, THE MAN ASKED, where do you take them? Oh, well, that's no problem, we said. There's any number of convenient one-day trips. You might start with. . .

He interrupted. He wanted to make it clear right now he wasn't interested in going out of town. He knew very well he could take them through Yosemite or through the Mother Lode and up to Sonora and Columbia or over to the dams and reservoirs or across the mountains to Monterey-Carmel or San Francisco.

None of the above, he said. They want to see our city, get an idea of what it's like. Maybe just a quick spin around to get the feel of the place. Where do you take them?

That's a different question, and not as easy. It depends on their interests and your interests.

You can always take them along I Street, under the arch, pointing over to City Hall and the Courthouse, to the McHenry Museum, the Library and the McHenry Mansion.

You can even tell them that they caught downtown in the middle of a renaissance and drive past the community center building site. You can show them the junior college and even visit the west campus if you want to throw in the thrill of venturing on the Briggsmore overpass.

In all of this, you need to remember what visitors usually find the most impressive about Modesto — the parks and the trees. That's why a drive down Sycamore Avenue past Graceada Park, over the canal and on out to Orangeburg is good.

Another good place for parks and trees is La Loma Avenue and a drive through there is a must, while it's still possible.

You might even cut across Morton Boulevard from there to Grand Street, then over the old bridge, but be very careful of that left turn. Then make the loop past the Gallo temple. If you're lucky, you may be able to show them a peacock or two strutting across the well kept lawn, but you will have to convince your visitors that you are indeed on the campus of the Gallo Winery, for nowhere will they see a sign.

If it is in the evening, you might go past the open door of the glass plant and watch the red hot bottles marching out of the molding machines.

Another possibility is a drive along River Road over to Mitchell Road, entering the city's back door across the bridge and around the airport. And watch out for that left turn, too. That route also provides an opportunity to show off a big portion of the city's industrial area.

If your visitors are interested in farms, we still have a few around. You can take them out Maze Road or Kiernan Avenue, and then by way of contrast, you might go over to Coffee or Old Oakdale Road and show them where all the peach orchards and walnut groves used to be. And out Scenic is still a nice drive, although not as scenic as it once was. But then, what is?

Of course, you can always go out to the Salida mall, depending, as we said, on your visitors' interests. People do like to go shopping in new places even though, if pressed, most people would admit that when you've seen one mall, you've seen them all.

Again, don't forget the trees. If you happen to be fortunate enough to have a friendly friend who lives in Ralston Tower, the view from the 11th floor is magnificent. You get a commanding sight of a veritable urban forest stretching out before you — hiding, softening, overhanging the harsh lines of the buildings. Trees of all kinds — the arching elms and tall sycamores, the sturdy old oaks and the stately, brooding deodar cedars with here and there the trim cypress sending its spike through the tree tops.

At night, the yellow lights of McHenry stretch out as far as the eye can see, and on Saturday night, the steady stream of cars, four abreast, make their ritualistic passage along the avenue.

On a clear night, off in the distance, you can see headlights climbing into the sky — stopping, starting, then disappearing almost like a line of lighted lemmings. What is it? What else?

The Briggsmore overpass.

—April 25, 1987

41

Works in progress

THE NEW STATUS REPORT ON MODESTO'S major public works projects was most helpful in bringing us up to date on where things stand. We had almost forgotten some of those things, but that's no wonder because a couple of them are barely alive.

Of primary interest is a plan to redesign the Briggsmore overpass (again), really an ominous prospect that deserves careful consideration. We'll get to that later.

The most encouraging development involves the city's transportation center. It has been in the works since 1975. Now the prospect is for completion by this time next year.

The plan would turn the old Southern Pacific depot on Ninth Street between I and K streets into a center for the city's buses, taxicabs, shuttles and other forms of transit, including Greyhound buses.

The old depot would be preserved and expanded, with the hope it would eventually serve its original purpose as a station for rail passengers. That's assuming the city will succeed in getting Amtrak to switch its San Joaquin trains to SP tracks, bringing them right into Modesto and Turlock instead of out in the country on Santa Fe tracks through Escalon, Riverbank, Empire and Denair.

However, it has been so long since this section of the SP has had passenger trains that there would be a good deal of clickety-clack on this route, possibly requiring slower speeds. And SP is not inclined to spend any great sums of money improving its road bed beyond what is required for freight traffic.

Also somewhat related is the longstanding effort to get the slow-moving Union Pacific trains off of Ninth Street and route them through the city on the SP tracks. Doug Carmody, the city's former parking and traffic director, has been working on this ever since we can remember and now, in semi-retirement, it is the only thing he is working on. He says maybe within a year we can have the long trains off Ninth Street. But he always was an optimistic guy.

The big bonus in this project is the plan to connect Kansas Avenue and Needham Street with an SP overpass at the north end of Ninth and to extend Tuolumne Boulevard under the trestles at the south end.

We are also fascinated with the idea of synchronizing all the city's traffic signals with a computer. We really are late in pursuing this needed improvement.

As for the performing arts theater at Modesto Centre Plaza, and as for a new police building, both have been laid low by a familiar ailment — no money. The theater was to be financed by public subscription, but there isn't a lot of that around anymore. The police building had been pinned on a couple of tax measures, neither of which was approved.

And the Lincoln-Lakewood bridge. We thought that proposal had died a number of years ago after the opponents presented an emotional slide show that kept the City Council up well past midnight.

We weren't sure whether the council buried the plan out of conviction or exhaustion, but the Public Works Department hasn't given up and wants it back on the capital improvement list.

Now, then, the Briggsmore overpass.

The proposal calls for a redesign to include adding a southbound on-ramp. Presumably that would help keep traffic on the existing on-ramp from backing up onto the highway during peak hours. Fine, but it probably would add another traffic light on the overpass.

What we really need on the Briggsmore overpass is an escape

ramp — a thing like they have on long down-grades to prevent runaways. Whenever a motorist got confused about which lane to be in or where to turn, he could pull onto the escape ramp. At the end of it would be a little parking plaza with telephones. The driver would be told how to start over and get where he wanted to go.

Or, if he stayed on the phone long enough, he would be told how to avoid the Briggsmore overpass altogether.

—May 2, 1992

Part III — Cancelling our Postmark: No, we haven't moved to Stockton

Where's our postmark?

IT WAS ONLY A MATTER OF TIME BEFORE our Bay Area friends got around to the matter of the mail. The all-too-innocent inquiries have started coming. The Stockton postmark was too much to pass up. Things like:

Do you actually drive up to Stockton to mail all your letters, or maybe you go there for dinner every night? We knew Mod-des-toh was growing but hadn't realized it reached Stockton. Now we know why that United flight from Moh-des-toh always stops in Stockton. And so on.

Have your fun, people, if it helps you while away the time when you are stalled bumper-to-bumper on the Nimitz Freeway during your twice daily commute. And occasionally remember that our refreshing walk to and from work takes exactly 14 minutes each way each day.

The truth of the matter is that the postmark is really an insufferable affront and an intolerable outrage. None of the explanations satisfy — greater efficiency, sophisticated technology, faster service.

When all is said and done, the loss of Modesto's postmark is a loss of Modesto's identity any way you pronounce it. There is just no way to explain why the mail from a city of almost 100,000 has to bear the postmark of a city in another county 30 miles away.

Why the City Council, the Chamber of Commerce, the Native Sons and Daughters, the historical societies, the stamp collectors, even the letter carriers have not raised unremitting hell about this fraudulent marking is a mystery. Somebody should be able to get elected to something on a "Restore Modesto's Postmark" platform. For that matter, how come John Thurman let this happen to us?

We can answer for the Briggsmore interchange by blaming it on our governor's lowered expectations or pretending the state sneaked it in while Doug Carmody was on vacation. We can brush off that mad maze of intersections around the city's official Christmas tree by claiming it is only temporary until the one-way streets are reversed again. But there just is no way to explain why a letter mailed in Modesto to a Modesto address must arrive with a Stockton postmark.

The post office here has an explanation, but it's easy to tell they don't care much for it either. In fact, when they get all done explaining how they don't have all the sophisticated equipment to handle the big volume of mail generated here, it is quite plain they don't like the Stockton postmark any more than we do.

And they are most eager to let you know they have a limited provision for a local postmark. There in one drop inside the main Kearney post office. Any letter deposited therein will be unfailingly imprinted with the rare and endangered Modesto postmark.

That's not good enough. It requires a special trip to the not-so-handy Kearney post office, and the drop is available only during regular business hours. Stick a letter in the box outside the post office and it will be on its way to Stockton.

Full restoration is the only answer. In the meantime, until a new leader emerges or John Thurman gets busy, the best temporary expedient in these days of do-it-yourself is to get a little rubber stamp made and affix your own Modesto postmark. Just like the postage meters do — for which we in Moh-des-toh bless their little automatic hearts.

—July 17, 1978

A limited comeback

TODAY MODESTO, TOMORROW THE WORLD! Our postmark is back. In limited form, yes, but don't knock it. For anybody who tuned in late, Postmaster Michael Austin announced last week that henceforth all letters with Modesto addresses that are mailed in any of four "local only" collection boxes will carry the Modesto post-mark.

Austin said he decided to provide this option as the result of favorable public comment on his earlier move to accommodate last-minute income tax filers. On that occasion the main post office

47

kept open until midnight to receive federal and state tax returns, all of which were given the Modesto postmark showing the very important deadline for mailing.

The limited return of the postmark is another responsive move on Austin's part and further evidence of increasing sensitivity to public attitudes. The announcement came in a mailed press release. It had no postmark. Not that it matters. It's just that we thought the postmaster passed up a good public relations opportunity to remind us of what the Modesto postmark looks like, considering its rarity.

Official federal mail hardly ever carries a postmark. It probably isn't needed. It's enough to know that we are hearing from the federal government. Usually the envelope has that printed post office logo with the eager eagle in place of a stamp with the warning that the penalty for private use to avoid payment of postage in $300.

Incidentally, that fine has been $300 for as long as we can remember. Postage has gone up but that fine has remained untouched. Nor have we ever heard of anybody being stuck with that penalty. Even most of the mail from our congressmen these days is quick to assure us that all the important information they are sending was not mailed at government expense. One of these days we should ask them at whose expense it is being mailed. Maybe we could save the congressmen some money.

Our wise friends in San Francisco thought the news about our postmark was hilarious. Or maybe "quaint" was the word they used.

Your letter about the big breakthrough arrived from Stockton, they said, and it's marvelous. Now you will be able to mail a letter to your neighbor across the street with full confidence that it will be postmarked from Modesto, provided you can find one of those four special mail boxes.

Well, that's San Francisco for you. They think anything that happens beyond their beloved Bay Area is frightfully amusing. Yet, when you get right down to it, there are probably no more provincial people on this side of the Hudson River. Look at all the flap over the city's "official" song. And now they're playing games with area codes. "In" things are 415 (their area code); "out" things are 408 (San Jose's area code). We're probably lucky they haven't discovered 209 yet.

Anyway, all their patronizing remarks were more than offset by a note from a longstanding well-wisher. It carried the Modesto postmark and arrived within two days of the announcement.

On the other hand, we did hear from a businessman who said he really didn't care what the post office stamped on his letters as long as they were delivered promptly to the right address.

As a taxpayer, he said he would rather have his money go for streamlining the operation to keep postal rates down than to spend it for restoring Modesto's postmark.

We have always maintained that all of our outgoing mail could readily be given a Modesto postmark at no increase in cost. Since all Modesto mail is already processed in a batch at the Stockton distribution center, all it would take would be a simple change of the dies on the cancelling machines. It is less bother, but not necessarily less costly, to do it the way it is now being done.

What all this really amounts to is one more step in homogenizing our identity and digitizing our individuality.

The more sophisticated our technology becomes, the more we seem to be turning everything into numbers. That's the computer influence, of course. Numbers are the language of the computer, but the genius of the machine is that it can quickly translate its language into our language, and we should keep insisting that it do so, even though it may be a little more trouble at times.

Otherwise, one of these days we'll all end up as bar codes.

Even San Franciscans might object to finding their song —
official or unofficial — had become: "I Left My Heart in 94101."

—*May 19, 1984*

Our landmark postmark

EVER SINCE THE U. S. POSTAL SERVICE issued an Elvis stamp,
we knew there was somebody in that organization with a heart.

But we never dreamed it would be quite so expansive. After all
these years of crusading and all but giving up the cause, we learn
that the grand old post office is ready to restore Modesto's postmark.

Modesto's Postmaster Mike Austin, who has always been sym-
pathetic to and helpful in this effort, deserves the credit for this victory.

He says within a couple of weeks, all mail originating in
Modesto will again be cancelled with the old Modesto postmark.

He did this by grabbing onto a piece of equipment that
became excess at the Stockton postal distribution center. It's called a
Mark II Facer Cancelor and it will allow him to cancel all mail and
put a Modesto postmark on it before it is shipped up to Stockton
for sorting and processing.

That's good news. For one thing, it means we can send out our
Christmas cards without having to worry about all the questions
from people who think we might have moved or who wonder why
we always go up to Stockton to mail our letters.

In fact, we had a friend in Portland who once sent an acknowl-
edgement saying, "I got this card postmarked in Stockton, but I
don't know anybody in Stockton, so I didn't open it."

It must be 20 years or so now since we have been grousing about the loss of our identity by the virtual elimination of our postmark, and we had just about given up seeing any change in our lifetime.

In the beginning, we wrote our congressmen and got the usual form letter in return, thanking us for our support and assuring us our representative was doing everything possible to hold the line on increased postage rates.

With the exception of B. F. Sisk, who was our congressman for a brief period between reapportionments. He sent a copy of a letter he had written to the Postmaster General calling attention to this matter and saying he would appreciate the general's personal effort to rectify this demeaning state of affairs.

Well, as far as we know, the general never did. But Sisk also sent us the name and telephone number of the post office official in Washington who was in charge of such things.

We called him, and he gave us the standard answer we had been getting from all the local officials. It's much more efficient to have a big regional center that cancels, processes and sorts all the mail and sends it on its way overnight, even if it means a letter to the guy across the street goes up to Stockton at night and comes back the next day.

We said, well, maybe, but wouldn't it be possible to change the postmark during that processing? He just laughed and said, "Listen, people don't care about that. I live in a little town outside of Washington, and I send out all my personal mail from there and it never carries my town's postmark, and that doesn't bother me at all. Out there in California, all those places around Los Angeles don't have their own postmarks as a rule — even Hollywood. It's mostly Los Angeles, Long Beach or Glendale.

We happen to know, however, that certain interests in

Hollywood did not take the loss of their postmark lying down and managed to wring a few concessions out of the postal service.

Much the same thing happened here.

During a tour of the Stockton regional distribution center one evening, we noticed that all the mail from Modesto arrived about the same time in big bulk lots and was dumped on a conveyor belt that sent it through the postmark and canceling machine. We wondered why it wouldn't be possible to change the plates on the canceling machine for that batch and then change them back again. The officials said it would take too much time and wasn't worth it.

Whereupon we proposed using a combination name for the postmark — taking the first four letters of Modesto and putting them together with the first three letters of Stockton to give us Mode-sto. That didn't get anywhere either.

So all our friends are saying, well, Cummerow, we got the postmark back. Now what are you going to write about?

Not to worry. There's always the trains on Ninth Street, Amtrak out in the country, a left-turn light for Orangeburg at McHenry, to name a few.

And there'll always be a Briggsmore overpass.

—*September 4, 1993*

Delivering the mail

IT'S TIME FOR AN UPDATE ON THE MODESTO postmark. Whatever happened to it? If you remember back in September of '93, we hailed the return of the Modesto postmark after some 20 years of telling people that we hadn't moved or really didn't go all the way up to Stockton to mail our letters

What happened then was that Modesto Postmaster Mike

Austin was browsing through the distribution center up in Stockton and he came across an old piece of surplus equipment that would allow him to put a Modesto postmark on all letters originating here before sending them up to Stockton to be sorted and sent on their way.

He brought it down here and began doing just that. But we did a little audit of our Christmas cards this year, and not a one of them had a Modesto postmark on it.

Most of them, which were obviously mailed from here, bore the old familiar Stockton postmark, but a dozen or so, which also obviously came from Modesto, were cancelled with a Sacramento postmark.

So what happened to our postmark? Mike said, with obvious disappointment and frustration, that it was a business decision.

Last fall some of the postal operations higher-ups came down here and took a look at what he was using to do it with. That stuff is too old, too slow and too obsolete to keep on using, they said.

They had the stuff hauled out and told him to go back to the old method of sending everything up to Stockton uncancelled. "But we managed to run 12 million letters through here with the Modesto postmark while it lasted," he said with pride.

And what about the Sacramento postmark?

Oh, that happens on weekends, Mike said. The Stockton center is also closed on weekends, so that anything that gets mailed from here after 5 p.m. Friday and all day Saturday gets sent up to Sacramento for processing.

In all this rejiggering, the postmaster did salvage one piece of equipment that allows him to put a Modesto postmark on mail for delivery in Modesto if it is dropped in a special box at the Kearney Avenue Main Post Office. He is now in the process of having that mail drop built into the partition at the post office.

MODESTO ON MY MIND

But Mike is not discouraged about the prospect for rebirth of the Modesto postmark.

He said the hope lies in the rapid advance of technology and the relatively short period of time before today's piece of smart machinery becomes obsolete and is replaced by much more sophisticated and versatile equipment.

He thinks that time is coming and with it will come the restoration of our postmark — as a good business decision.

January 7, 1995

Part IV — Wink Van Ripple: The old timer wakes up every 20 years or so and wonders whatever happened to Modesto

A brief awakening

TWENTY YEARS AGO WINK VAN RIPPLE fell asleep during a Forward Modesto committee meeting. He was awakened two days ago and headed straight for the civic auditorium.

For more than four hours he went from one location to another, pausing frequently in confusion until he glimpsed a familiar sight, then moving off in another direction.

"I give up," he said at last. "Where did you put it?"

Wink never waited for an answer to anything. He seemed to be on another wavelength, as though the transmit button were stuck; he could send, but he couldn't receive.

He picked up only one clue. "They told me there used to be a sign down there where the Lincoln School was," he said. "Must have been a terrible earthquake."

There wasn't any earthquake, Wink.

"Twice I thought I'd found the auditorium," he went on. "That big new building across from what's left of the courthouse. I went in there and asked a woman if it was the auditorium. She said they didn't have any room in there for an auditorium. In fact, she said they didn't have any room in there for the assessor. Such a nice new building, too. Running water and everything.

"Thought I'd found it when I came to that big white building with the wrap-around front porch. Would have made a good auditorium, but somebody filled it up with books and magazines and arty pictures."

He couldn't get over the Lincoln School. "Such a pretty little school. That must have been a bad storm."

There wasn't any storm, Wink.

"Even killed most of the trees. The ones that's left are pretty sad looking. Must have wiped out that nice old church, too. But I can't figure out why the Episcopals would put up such a tall building."

The Episcopalians have a new church, Wink. That tall building is Ralston Tower.

"I guess it's like my mother used to say, though, it won't hurt the Episcopals to get as close to heaven as they can while they're on earth."

They're doing quite well, Wink.

"And the Presbyterians. Instead of rebuilding the church, looks like they went into business on that corner.

The church sold that property, Wink, and moved to a north location.

"Either that or they moved out. My mother used to say whenever the going got rough, you could always count on the Presbyterians to get out."

You had a very ecumenical mother, Wink.

The hardest thing for him to recognize was downtown.

"If it hadn't been for Penney's, I would have been lost. But that's a good solid building. Take a mighty strong hurricane to do that one in."

There wasn't any hurricane, Wink.

"They must have lost that manager they had. He was a good one. Lot of people thought he was grumpy, but that's because they didn't know him. He was a square shooter and knew his business. One of J.C.'s boys."

J.C.'s nephew, Wink, and he retired. But there's good news on the building. Some local men bought it, and they're going to fix it all up into offices. Be a real help to downtown.

"Can't believe one of J.C.'s boys would let the inventory run down like that."

Something else was bothering Wink.

"I know what's missing," he exclaimed. "The old Capital School. That's gone, too, and *The Bee* went to such great pains to save it."

And did for quite a while, Wink, but they just had to make room for a bigger press.

"Paper's changed, too. Notice that? Great big headlines on the front page. And they even tell you when you get to the back page. But that's not really the back page. The back page used to be the editorial page. They've moved that, too, so now you come to it without any warning. Used to be you could put it face down, like a hole card, and bring it up close to get a little look at it before you turned it over. Everything's changed. Must have been quite a twister ripped through here."

There wasn't any twister, Wink.

"Can't figure where they could have put that auditorium."

We're still working on it, Wink. It was looking pretty good there for a while. Then there was this Proposition 13 on the ballot, and under Prop. 13, Wink, the people said the state and federal governments are spending too much money, so we're going to limit the amount local governments can take and then ... Wink ...

He was asleep again.

—*September 23, 1978*

Wink's waking hours

EVERYBODY SURELY REMEMBERS WINK Van Ripple. He fell asleep 20 years ago near Modesto Junior College. It happened while he was waiting for the traffic light to change at Stoddard and College Avenues.

Wink awoke last year and hasn't slept since. Not a wink, as he is fond of saying. And furthermore, he says, he won't rest until he gets this matter settled.

He is doing battle with the state sales tax people. He went out to buy a bag of fertilizer, and the man wanted to know what he wanted it for. Wink told him it was none of his danged business, but the man said it was necessary so he'd know whether or not to charge sales tax. Lawn, Wink snapped. The man added 6 percent.

"Regulation 1588 says fertilizer for a vegetable garden is tax exempt but for a lawn is taxable," the man said, reading from a green paper.

Wink took a look. "Aha! It also says here that tax does not apply to sales of fertilizer to be applied to land the products of which will be used to feed livestock of the kind the products of which ordinarily constitute food for human consumption."

Who eats grass, the man wanted to know.

"My nanny goat, that's who," Wink said. "And I milk her and if everything keeps going up, I may have to eat the poor critter. No tax."

The man hesitated. "It says here I got to get a certificate in writing that the fertilizer will be used in an exempt manner. Got to have your name, address, signature, seller's permit number or reason you do not have a seller's permit."

Wink blinked. "Forget the fertilizer," he said. "Just give me that copy of Regulation 1588. I'll feed that to nanny, and we'll all be ahead." He walked out.

Wink had other complaints. "You got yourself a skin-tight society," he said. What did he mean by that?.

"Ever buy any hardware," he asked. "I got hardware all over my house. Can't get it open. It's all on these cards. Pretty as a picture. I can see it. I can touch it, but I can't get at it."

Skin packs. That's what he was talking about. They are hard to open.

"Hardware's all molded into this stuff that's tougher'n cat gut. Can't get through it. Always got to buy more than you need. Things you need two pairs of comes in threes. Things you need in threes comes in fives. Can't get one of anything anymore. It's a skin-tight society."

As you know, Wink is fine tuned. He only receives when the vibrations are right.

"People are getting packed in like that, too," he went on. "They're all getting pulled into themselves, and you can't get at them. Things like "Fill the Dam" or "Dam the Fill," " Truck the Crops" or "Crop the Trucks." Everything is one thing or the other. My mother used to say a human being is like a fine timepiece, and neither one should get wound up too tight."

Wink himself was getting a little wound up. Better change the subject.

Has he been reading anything interesting lately.

"Been reading a lot of things. Newspapers, magazines, a lot of things."

Anything interesting?

"Don't really know," Wink snapped. "Never been able to finish any of them."

Yes, well, he has been rather busy. Trying to buy fertilizer, stocking up on hardware, that kind of thing.

"Not because I've been too busy, either," he continued. "It's because I've never been able to find the end of anything. I finish one page of a magazine, and at the end it tells me to please turn to page 64. I'd be pleased to turn to page 64 if I could find it. They got all kinds of pages in between with no numbers on them. They got pages with everything from A64 to Z64 but no plain 64. Never have found it. Don't believe it's there."

Yes, that is annoying. Some magazines do have funny numbering systems. Hard to follow.

"And your paper isn't a whole lot better. Tells you to turn to the back page or look on B-2, and you can look for the rest of the morning and you'll never find any more."

Occasionally it does get puzzling.

"Puzzles, too. Some days you have a puzzle that says the answer will appear tomorrow. Tomorrow comes and there's no answer. My mother used to say yesterday's gone forever and tomorrow may never come, so you better make use of the here and now."

Wink's mother was full of wise sayings. And other things. She also drank a lot. But those newspaper slip-ups are relatively rare and easily explained. You see, what happens is that each page is put together separately, and when a story goes from one page to another, it has to be cut off and taken over ...

Wink blinked and nodded. He was asleep again.

—June 30, 1979

A midwinter night's dream

OUR OLD FRIEND WINK VAN RIPPLE woke up again the other day and declared that he may never go to sleep again. He was still shaking. He said he'd had this bad dream — just one long series of nightmares that seemed to go on for 20 years.

Wink said at the beginning of the dream, he was driving out G Street in search of Scenic Drive. He said he could remember having found it once going that way, but the next time he tried he wound up on Rue de Yoe, and had never been able to locate Scenic again.

In the dream, he didn't even get close. He was going along when the city suddenly decided to reverse the flow of traffic. Right before his eyes, all the one-way arrows began flipping over and pointing in the opposite direction. Wink looked up to see three lanes of traffic bearing down on him. He narrowly made it to the next cross street and turned in just as the platoon of traffic roared by. It frightened him just to recall it.

We reminded him that it was only a dream. The funny thing, though, is that the city had been thinking about turning G Street traffic around, but finally settled on a much simpler plan. It will just get rid of any two-way traffic on Downey Street and do a much more effective job of hiding Scenic Drive.

Wink said he was so shaken, he parked the car and walked home. After he settled down a bit, he began going through the mail and found a letter from Newport Beach. It looked official and ominous. And it was. It was a notice to pay an overtime parking ticket within five days or face dire consequences.

The old timer scratched his head. He had never been in Newport Beach. Must be a mistake. He tossed the notice in the wastebasket and headed out to see if the dog needed water. More trouble. The gate was open. Darn dog got out again. He went back in, put on his coat and started out to look for the dog. When he opened the front door, there was an officer standing on the porch writing out a citation for violation of the leash law.

Having left his car over near G Street somewhere, Wink started out on foot. He hadn't gone two blocks when he was attacked by a vicious pit bull and severely bitten. Never, in all this dream, was there ever anybody around to help him. He finally managed to beat off the dog and began hobbling to the nearest hospital.

When he entered, he was stopped by a man and asked to show his American Express card. Wink offered him a Visa or a Master Card, but the man said, no, only American Express. He advised him to try the hospital down the road. When he got to the next place, the woman was apologetic but firm. They didn't accept any credit cards, she said, but they did give a 10 percent discount to senior citizens.

By the time Wink got to the third hospital, an officer was waiting for him. He had Wink treated, then took him to the county jail where was booked for failure to appear in court on the leash law violation, fingerprinted, strip-searched and locked up.

Wink said he couldn't remember how he got of jail, but somehow or other he was set free and he headed home. As he neared the house, he saw all these flashing red lights and his heart sank. A SWAT team had surrounded his place, and several heavily armed men were moving furtively from tree to tree.

He must have broken out of jail, we suggested, and the men were after him. No, Wink said, it was that Newport Beach parking ticket. The computer put out a warrant for him. But the nightmare was over. He woke up when a trooper pointed a machine gun at him and hollered "Freeze!" He was still shaken.

Well, we reminded him again that it was just a dream. We thought it might cheer him up a little to tell him that, by coincidence, the city is reworking the leash law to crack down on vicious dogs.

Wink thought that was a good idea. He said the law should be as tough on dogs as it is on people.

—February 11, 1984

All in favor...

OLD WINK VAN RIPPLE WOKE UP AGAIN, rubbed his eyes and looked around. He wanted to know when the bomb hit.

There was no bomb. This is the site of our new community center. He wanted to know when we moved it.

We started to tell him it was about 10 years ago, but Wink has a habit of not waiting for answers. Last time he heard it was going to be on the other side of the tracks, near St. Stanislaus Church. Before that it was going to be on H Street somewhere or maybe near the freeway.

Once they got as far as putting up a sign out there where the old tile-roof school was, Wink recalled. That was Lincoln School, we said.

Wink looked around and wanted to know where all the merchants went. We told him all about the mall out near Beckwith Road.

Beckwith Road? Wink thought about that a minute and then chuckled. You mean they all just picked up and moved out to Salida, eh? He chuckled again. Well, why not, he said. That's the way this town started, you know. Now there was no stopping him.

Wasn't a thing here except some wheat and jackrabbits, he said, until the Central Pacific railroad came through. People settled along the river at places like Paradise and Empire City. Then when the tracks came through, they just picked up their businesses and moved them along the tracks. That's how Modesto got started, practically overnight. People will do that, you know. They want to be where the action is.

Yes, Wink. We knew he was going to tell us again that it must really be something when people will leave Paradise and move to Modesto, and he did. They didn't have much of a community center in those days either, he went on. The closest thing was a saloon on Front Street. But the ladies didn't much care for that. Wink wanted to know about this community center. Are the folks in favor of it?

We told him it was hard to say. He would have to find out for himself. Wink liked to do that anyway — stop people on the street and find out what they are thinking — except that he usually did more talking than listening.

Wink said he would see us later and headed off up the street.

Later in the day he returned with a startling announcement. Everybody's for it, he said. Then he changed it a little. He said he ran into only one man who was dead set against it. And even he said he didn't have anything against the community center personally, it was just that 20 years ago he wanted to have a yard sale at his house every Tuesday, Thursday and Saturday, and the city wouldn't let him. Ever since, everything the city has been for, including tree planting, he's been against.

Otherwise, Wink said, everybody he talked to is in favor of a community center — but not necessarily this one. One fellow says he likes everything but the hotel. He said the city doesn't need a hotel there, and besides he has a better place for a hotel out near Salida somewhere.

Wink said another citizen who was very strong for a community center said it was high time the city stopped talking about it and started doing something. But he said there was no need to go to all this trouble. The city could go right out to Woodland Avenue and take over the old FMC plant. It's just sitting out there not doing a thing, he said.

Then there was another who favored the center, but he thought we should build phase 2 before we build phase 1. He said we need those theaters more than we need that other stuff, and we ought to get first what we need most.

Next Wink said he ran into this vigorous young man in a gym suit. He was very enthusiastic about the community center. It was an excellent plan in a good location and he backed it a thousand percent — if we could just get them to change that conference center into a sports arena.

We tried to tell Wink that this is exactly how we got where we are, but he was beginning to nod again. For all these years everybody has agreed that we need a good community center, yet when we got right down to the nitty-gritty we ran into all of these people who were in favor of a community center — but not this one. Instead of putting it here, we should put it over there; instead of having this, we should have that; instead of having the city do it, we should let private enterprise do it. And so forth. The result, after all these years, is that we have nothing.

Wink's eyes were closed. We shook him gently and asked him what we should do.

He opened one eye and looked up. Maybe, he said, we should all pack up and move back to Paradise.

—*October 19, 1985*

The library that was

WE WERE WALKING OUT I STREET WITH our old friend, Wink Van Ripple, and he was marveling at all the changes in the last 20 years. Hardly know the place, he said. It was in the fall of the year, and the leaves were beginning to turn.

Wink stopped at a construction site and wanted to know what was going on. They finally getting around to replacing the old school? No, no. The school has been gone for a long time. This is the new *Bee* building. The new what? The new *Bee* building. Wink scratched his head. Oh, he said, without any sign of recognition.

The radio station, he asked. Where's the radio station? That's out near Modesto Junior College West. West? Wink echoed. You mean they've got an East and a West now. Yes. West is out on Blue Gum Avenue. Wink nodded. Out near the state hospital, he said. No, that is the state hospital — or where the state hospital was. No more state hospital? Wink couldn't believe it. How can you get along without a state hospital? We had no answer.

He was still eying the construction. Where did the delicatessen go? The delicatessen closed and turned into a parking lot. He couldn't imagine giving up that mouth-watering aroma and doing without Elmo's ravioli. And the lawyers? They're over on 12th

Street. The doctors? They moved out, too.

Wink shook his head. It may be progress, he said, but that sure seems like a lot of space to devote to bees. We moved on up the street.

At least the library looks good, he said. That's not the library. It used to be the library. Now it's the McHenry Museum. They have some wonderful historical collections and exhibits and other reminders of how things used to be. Wink said he didn't need any reminders. He remembered how things used to be, and he remembered when that was the library. The books were packed in there from floor to ceiling. It was crowded and cramped, and people could hardly get in and out of the place.

Well, now. We built a much more spacious library. Takes up a full block. It offers a lot more in the way of books, periodicals, reference materials, audio-visual aids and it houses the county's central library system. Good, Wink said, he was glad to see there had been some progress, and we continued on up the street.

When we got to the corner, Wink stopped. What's this? This, we told him is the new library. What happened to it? Did they have a fire? The building was dark. The flags weren't flying. Nobody was coming or going. Cobwebs were beginning to span the space between the massive columns.

The library is still operating, we told him, but it is now open only on Tuesday from noon to 5. Wink wanted to make sure he had this straight. The other library was much too small, so we built this big new one and then closed it six days a week?

We explained the situation. The county ran out of money and said it could no longer afford to fund the library. It wanted the cities to take over. The cities agreed to chip in for one year, but said they couldn't afford to keep on doing it forever. So the cities and county got together and decided to seek a special tax that would go totally to the full funding of the library system. Then in August we had this election.

What happened? Wink waited. Well, nobody seemed to be in charge. The Friends of the Library did their best to organize a campaign, but the libraries themselves couldn't promote the effort, and the nine cities never got together to stress the importance of the election to the future of the library. Nobody seemed to realize how drastic the cuts would be unless the tax was approved.

Wink nodded. And the people turned it down, he said. Well, more people voted for than voted against it, but not enough more. It needed two "yes" votes for every "no" vote because it was one of those two-thirds propositions.

How much was the tax? It was $34 per household per year.

No wonder, Wink said. That could mean passing up one movie a month or maybe foregoing one weekend trip during the year. It might even hurt the Lottery.

—June 28, 1986

Rail progress

OUR OLD FRIEND WINK VAN RIPPLE woke up again and wanted to know what all the excitement was about in Sacramento.

He thought maybe there had been some new find at Sutter's Mill. We told him no, nothing like that. Sacramento simply has been celebrating the advent of a new and modern transportation system.

Wink was a little wary. Don't tell me they have moving sidewalks or flying automobiles or pneumatic people-movers.

No, nothing like that, either, Wink. They now have street cars.

Street cars! What's new about that? We had street cars 40 years ago.

Well, they aren't exactly street cars. They call it light rail.

Light rail? Wink repeated. Do they have tracks? Yes. Do they have a trolley? Yes. Do they have a motorman? Yes. Do they have a bell? Yes. They're street cars, Wink said, and that settled that.

And certainly, Wink said, they're not new. Never could figure out why all the cities were in such a hurry to tear up perfectly good trolley systems.

Had to make room for the buses. Buses are more flexible.

Oh, they're more flexible all right, Wink agreed. And noisier and smellier and jerkier. They clog up the streets, they break down and they cost more to operate.

O.K., so we made a mistake. We're trying to correct it. We have to do something. The highway people say we don't have enough money to build all the roads we need, and even if we did have, we couldn't build enough roads to take care of all the traffic we're going to have by the end of the century.

Never should have torn up all those tracks, Wink repeated, shaking his head. Just look at the Bay Area. Once upon a time there wasn't a place you couldn't get to on a street car or one of those big Key System trains. Those trains went right over the Bay Bridge into a big terminal in San Francisco. You hopped on a street car and got where you were going. Maybe you had to transfer to a cable car, but that was no problem. Cable cars were taking people to work then, not hauling tourists down to Fishermen's Wharf. They tore up that whole system and took the tracks off the bridge to make more room for automobiles, and now they have more cars than they can handle and no place to park them when they get there.

Oh, but we have BART now.

Wink was ready for that. Sure, he said, after they woke up and realized what they'd done, they spent a few hundred million dollars trying to fix it. But they still haven't fixed it. Two places people in San Francisco want to get are Marin County and the airport.

69

BART doesn't go to either one of those. It probably won't be too long before they rediscover ferries.

But they still have street cars in San Francisco.

Just a token, Wink said. They don't have five pairs of tracks running down Market Street like they used to.

True, but that's about all they don't have running down Market Street.

Wink wanted to know if we had any grand plan to bring back street cars here.

Nothing firm, we told him. We are still too busy trying to get the trains off Ninth Street.

He was alarmed. You mean you're going to tear up those tracks?

Not necessarily, we just want to get rid of the trains, not the tracks. There is a possibility those tracks might eventually provide us with a light rail link to Turlock and Stockton.

You mean street cars, Wink pressed.

If you prefer. Good idea, Wink said. You could go to the college or Del Rio — maybe even get to French Camp International Airport that way.

Wink yawned. He wanted to get back to sleep, but with all these new-fangled ideas on the horizon, he had one piece of advice.

Don't let them tear down any livery stables.

—March 14, 1987

Building for tomorrow

WINK VAN RIPPLE AWAKENED, LOOKED around and wanted to know what was going on over at what he called the Sentry Plaza. We told him there was probably something of a celebration in progress.

He couldn't figure out why they would be celebrating when the place isn't even done yet. That part of it is done, we told him. Couldn't be, he said, most of the front part where the fountain comes on now and then was roped off.

Well, that's something else. That part is closed off until they put a wheelchair ramp in. Should have thought of that in the first place, Wink said. We told him that's what the Attorney General said. Smart man, that Ed Meese, he said. We started to correct him and then remembered that he doesn't really care about those kinds of details.

So what was all the excitement about, he wanted to know. We said we presumed they were celebrating the fact that they got a unanimous vote on a matter involving the community center.

Unanimous? Wink blinked in disbelief. All seven of them? No, six. John Sutton couldn't be at the meeting.

And what about Mayor Mensinger, he went on, she couldn't vote either. She's not mayor anymore, Wink. She stepped down last year.

What's she doing now? She's out after the county. Wink was listening now. Spreading her wings, eh? That's good. She'll give them something to think about. Another Measure A, maybe. Well, yes, you could say that.

Wink still couldn't believe it. You mean to tell me Patterson voted for this thing? he asked. Yes, he did. He said things had reached the point where he had to vote for it to save the city.

71

And McGrath? He couldn't have voted for it. He was voting against it before he was even on the council. Nevertheless, he went along.

Wink rubbed his eyes. Hard to follow, he said. Just what was this thing they were voting for?

They were voting for the hotel.

Oh, sure, Wink said. Of course. John Q. Hammons. He's not too good on parking garages, but you don't have to worry. You already have that. He'll build you a nice all-suite hotel.

It's not going to be an all-suite hotel, Wink. It's going to be a regular hotel. And John Q. Hammons isn't going to build it. Allen Grant is going to build it.

Allen Grant. That name sounds familiar. Let's see now. Oh, yeah. He's the auto dealer, right?

Well, we're not quite sure about that yet, Wink, but we do know he's a developer.

Sure, and he'll put up a nice Quality Inn for you. All suites.

No, Wink, it's not going to be all suites, and it's not going to be a Quality Inn. It's going to be a Red Lion Hotel.

That's fine, Wink said, not really listening. And the 10-story office building. When's that going up?

There isn't going to be any office building.

No office building? How come?

It's this way. When John Q. Hammons decided to switch to an all-suite hotel, the footprint was too big to allow space for the office building, and besides, the financing for office buildings dried up.

Yes, we did say Hammons isn't going to build it. But when Allen Grant took over, he planned to have an all-suite hotel. Later, he decided we'd be better off with an 11-story regular hotel.

11-story hotel, eh? Wink thought about that. And no offices?

Not exactly. We're going to have some offices. Allen Grant got to thinking about it and decided to make the top two floors into offices.

So, you're going to have a 9-story hotel and two floors of offices.

No, no. That was an 11-story hotel plus two floors of offices.

So then you're going to have a 13-story building, Wink said.

Actually, it's going to be a 15-story building. Allen Grant later decided to put up an 11-story hotel plus four floors of offices at the top.

Wink was losing interest. He looked around and yawned.

Finally, he said he could understand why we got a unanimous vote. He could even see why Patterson and McGrath voted for it. They had to do something, he said.

That building was just getting too high.

—*May 21, 1988*

It's festival time

WINK VAN RIPPLE WOKE UP AND looked down I Street. He couldn't believe his eyes. He shook his head and said he never thought he'd see the day.

In the olden days, he said, they never would have let them get away with that — put up a circus right in the middle of downtown.

They'd let them parade through downtown, but they'd have to go out of town for the circus itself. Seems to me they used to send them out on Seventh Street, out there near the auction yard. Never right smack dab in the middle of downtown.

It's not a circus, Wink.

Not a circus? Then it must be a revival meeting. They used to make them go out of town, too. We had one here that ran for near-

73

ly a month. Great big tent, and people would come from all over every night. They did a big business out there — only they didn't like for you to call it a business. Now they're putting it on right in the middle of downtown. The Lord sure does work in mysterious ways.

It's not a revival meeting, Wink.

It's got to be either a circus or a revival meeting.

No, it's a food festival.

A food festival? You mean the Farmers Market has gotten that big? I hate to see them move from 16th Street. They were in that block between the Methodist Church and the library. That's a good location. They have faith on one side and knowledge on the other.

The Farmers Market is still there, Wink, and this isn't a Farmers Market. It's a food festival — they're going to have prepared food and refreshments and music and entertainment and booths and a car show and all kinds of things. It's called Modesto ala Carte.

Modesto ala Carte? That means you can order anything you want. Sort of like a big picnic in a tent.

Wink still didn't understand it. You have all these nice parks, and you have that big new Sentry Plaza right down the street, and you put up all these big tents right smack dab in the middle of downtown.

They're not exactly tents, Wink. They're more like canopies. We're trying to recapture the idea of a hometown celebration. We have to do something. Riverbank has wine and cheese, Stockton has asparagus, Gilroy has garlic, Hilmar has cows, Patterson has apricots, Ripon has almonds and Turlock has the fair.

Wink allowed as how it was all right, but he said it was going to be a mess tonight. When the young ones start dragging 10th and 11th Streets, you're going to have your hands full.

They don't drag 10th and 11th anymore, Wink.

They don't? Wink frowned. That's a shame. That was something to see. With 10th and 11th being one-way streets, it was ideal.

They aren't one-way streets anymore, Wink.

They aren't? That's too bad. Every Friday and Saturday night they'd make the loop through downtown — out on 11th Street and back on 10th. Occasionally, they would duck out and go over to Burge's Drive-In on Ninth Street. You should have seen them. Three abreast, moving along the street. All those cars and all those antics. Somebody should have made a movie about it.

Somebody did. George Lucas made the film. It was called "American Graffiti," and that's what all this is a part of. Every year at this time, right after graduation, we have Graffiti Night, and this year Modesto ala Carte is part of that.

George Lucas, eh? Wink interrupted. I know George Lucas. He's the fellow that has that stationery store there.

No, that's the father. George Lucas, the son, made the movie.

Made the movie right here in Modesto, Wink marveled. That must have been something.

Well, not exactly. The movie wasn't made in Modesto. It was made in Petaluma.

Petaluma! Wink was aghast. Why would they make a movie about Modesto in Petaluma?

Because by the time they made the movie, Petaluma's downtown looked more like Modesto's downtown used to look than Modesto's did.

Wink could understand that. He yawned and said he was beginning to have trouble recognizing Modesto's downtown.

Too many tents.

June 17, 1989

Ahead to the past

WINK VAN RIPPLE WOKE UP AGAIN and wondered where he was. You're in Modesto, Wink, we told him. Modesto, California.

Can't be, he said. Thought I just felt some rain. You did, Wink, and it's about the first we've had since you fell asleep.

Can't be as bad as that, he said. It's still pretty green around here.

For now, yes, but we're heading into our seventh year of drought. We got a little rain but not nearly enough, and it could be really dry next summer.

Yeah, Wink said. I run into one of them fellers from the East who was crabbing about California's weather. He said it's always the same, either green or brown. You don't have but two seasons — hot or cold — and worst of all, you don't get the fall colors.

I told him he didn't know what he was talking about. Take a ride out College Avenue, I told him, and you'll think you're in New England. The street is ablaze with color.

You got your buttery yellow ginkgo trees, some liquidambar that's turning yellow and red, the spectacular Chinese pistache coming out with a fiery red, and even the Modesto ash is beginning to drop its golden carpet. What's he mean, we don't get any color? Just because we don't have many maple trees and those we do have don't do much doesn't mean we don't have color. We have other trees that put on a real fall show. I told him to go out to that Sisters Park and open his eyes.

That's Graceada Park, Wink. And calm down. These interlopers from the East have to have something to cling to. You seldom hear them bragging about all the snow and sleet and slush and sub-freezing weather they have. Considering the weather around the county this year — hurricanes and floods and tornadoes — we've been pretty lucky.

Wink agreed. Then he wanted to know where we were. We told him downtown.

Downtown, he said. Can't be. This is December, isn't it?

Yes, it's getting close to Christmas.

Can't be. Where's all the Christmas lights?

We don't light up downtown like we used to anymore.

Where's Sears?

Gone.

Where's Penney's? Gone.

Loeb's? Gone. Musser's? Just left. Even Topper's is gone. How about the Covell? They still having all those Christmas parties downstairs in the Fable Room? They used to have a great restaurant there.

None of that's happening anymore, Wink. Even the theater is closed.

Wink looked downcast. Then he brightened and said, I know, they've all packed up and moved out to Machinery Village. Nice place out there. They have Joseph Magnin and Dunlap's and Roos-Atkins and lots of places.

That's McHenry Village, Wink, and none of those places are there anymore.

Wink wasn't listening. About the only thing out there you might recognize, Wink, are Carmen's and maybe Keller's.

Keller's, he said. You don't mean that little variety store across from Roosevelt School?

That's right. But it's no little variety store anymore. It's quite a large and high quality gift store that's always cheerfully and tastefully decorated. They attract shoppers from miles away.

I believe it, Wink said. They used to have good penny candy over by Roosevelt.

77

So where did everybody go? Well, all the big places — Sears and Penney's plus Macy's and Weinstock's and Gottschalk's went out to Vintage Faire.

Vintage Faire? Oh, you mean the Salida Mall, he said. Why would anybody go all the way to Salida unless it was for almonds?

Dunno, Wink. Dunno. But they go out there in droves from all over the place. They have acres of parking out there, and it's hard to find one close to the stores. One of these days they're going to have to put in an elephant train.

Wink was getting sleepy. Well, if it gets too crowded out there, some of them could move back downtown. Sears and Penney's could come back, and we could put up the lights again and build more parking places and ...

Not likely. But who knows?

Wink dozed off again.

—December 5, 1992

Waking up to reality

WINK VAN RIPPLE AWAKENED SUDDENLY after a long sleep, and this time he found himself up on the knoll in front of Modesto Centre Plaza next to the main fountain.

He rubbed his eyes and looked around.

He saw the parking lot jammed with cars, people streaming in the main entrance and others making their way to the Red Lion Hotel.

This Sentry Plaza sure is busy, he said as he scanned the scene. They must be making a lot of money here.

Well, not exactly, Wink.

You see, it's not their purpose to make money. They're mainly trying to encourage people to use this place, and they're doing pretty well with that. The city has to chunk in a little money every year to pay the bills. But compared to a lot of other cities, it's not costing them much.

This year they figure it will take $380,000, including the subsidy for the parking garage across the street. That's about 31 percent of what it costs to operate this place.

You take Sacramento. It costs them $5 million a year to operate their center, and they kick in $3.3 million. That's 66 percent.

Almost the same with Fresno. Theirs also costs $5 million a year, and they pay out $2.7 million or 54 percent.

Wink figured it was probably well worth it.

You're getting a lot of new businesses to open up around here, aren't you?

We looked down at the ground. Sort of. We have a bunch of new restaurants on 10th Street and then there is Sweetwater's and St. Stan's across from the parking garage.

But there's some bad news, too.

Woolworth's, a few doors down the street, is going to close.

Wink was wide awake.

Woolworth's, he echoed. They can't do that. Where am I going to eat? Where am I going to get my gummi-bears? They're doing a good business in there. How come they're closing?

You just can't tell about these chains, Wink. They're all downsizing and it's probably a decision made by a computer. If their volume isn't up to some arbitrary figure, they go on the hit list.

It's just like the Piccadilly Restaurant out there in McHenry Village. They seemed to be doing a good business, and all of sudden they decide to give up the ghost, and within a couple of weeks they were out of there.

On the other hand, downtown there is the Piccadilly Deli — which had the name first in our book. They were doing a good business, so they moved down the street a couple of doors into larger quarters, and they're doing a better business.

They serve good food at reasonable prices with good, fast service. Besides, they're the place that sold a lottery ticket to the Rev. Warren Lawson that got him a chance on the Big Spin.

The Rev. Lawson, Wink repeated. A man of the cloth playing the lottery?

Yes, he got a little static about that. When his neighbor read about it, he came over to scold him.

Warren told him that if the Lord hadn't wanted religious people to gamble a little he wouldn't have created Bingo.

That didn't satisfy his neighbor. He wanted to know where Warren had bought the ticket.

Warren saw a chance to have a little fun and run his neighbor off at the same time. He told him he got it from a machine in the basement of the Baptist church.

We all know that's not true, that the Baptists don't have lottery machines, but it worked and his neighbor went off muttering to himself and shaking his head.

This Rev. Lawson, Wink asked, what church does he have?

He doesn't have any at the moment. He just preaches to the Sons in Retirement every chance he gets, and that's probably as challenging a congregation as he could find anywhere. His biggest problem is trying to keep them from falling asleep.

Yep, Wink agreed. It's no easy job trying to get people to stay awake.

And he fell sound asleep again.

—*October 23, 1993*

The way we were

OLD WINK VAN RIPPLE WOKE UP AGAIN and couldn't figure out where he was. You're in Modesto, we told him. He said he knew that, but where? He looked around and didn't recognize anything.

Actually, you are just about in the center of Modesto, we said. You're sitting on a bench in front of the Courthouse at 11th and I Streets. Look behind you.

He did, then turned back around shaking his head sadly. Yep, that's the Courthouse. But are they still holding court there?

Every day. People come in to serve on juries, they try cases and render verdicts. Just like always.

Well, Wink said, it's about the only thing that's just like always. Don't recognize much else around this corner.

Didn't recognize much else? What did he mean.

Take a look, he said. Over there, the Copper Kettle's gone. All we have is a couple of hot dog stands in front of here. Bank of America is no longer on this corner or the one up above. Even Nichol News is gone. Across the street, Lowery's gift shop is missing and even L. M. Morris is gone.

But the post office is still there, Wink.

Yes, he agreed, it's nice to know the main post office is still downtown.

We almost hated to tell him. That's not the main post office anymore, Wink. The main post office is out on Kearney Avenue. This is El Viejo Station.

El Viejo? What's that mean?

It means the old one, we told him.

The old one, he repeated. Well, it's just about the only El Viejo downtown. You lost Penney's, you lost Sears, you lost Loeb's, you lost Woolworth's and now they're monkeying around with the

81

Hotel Covell. The trouble with Modesto, he said, is it doesn't have any center anymore.

What do you mean, we asked. What about Centre Plaza. That place is buzzing with activity. Wink said he knew all about Sentry Plaza, but it still hadn't pulled everything together downtown.

You build a great transportation center around the old Southern Pacific depot, he said. It has buses, it has taxicabs, it has shuttles, it has everything except trains. And now instead of bringing trains into the fine new station, you're talking about taking the station out to the trains. You're going to put up a depot along the Santa Fe tracks out near Village One.

And that's another thing, Wink said. You're stretching Modesto out in all directions. No wonder it doesn't have a center. You've got a big mall out in Salida, you're moving the welfare office and the jail out to Ceres, you put the juvenile justice center out near the west campus of Modesto Junior College, and you still haven't got the trains off Ninth Street.

Hold on, Wink. We aren't responsible for all those things. The county has some responsibility. And we have the word of Doug Carmody that the days of the trains on Ninth are numbered.

Be that as it may, Wink said, most of the great names of Modesto's trade and commerce have disappeared.

That's true, we conceded, but a good many remain.

Name one, Wink challenged.

Well, we couldn't begin to remember them all, but there's Charley Madonna's Liquor Store on H Street, there's Dan Mellis Liquors at a number of locations, there's Zagaris Realty and Max Foster's Farms.

Foster Farms? Wink repeated. He's down in Livingston. Well, yes, but his original close ties are with us. Then there's Lyng's Feed & Seed, Fred Hill Plumbing, Fregoso's El Faro Restaurant, Storer

Transportation Service and Loeb's Department Store.

Wait a minute, Wink said. Loeb's isn't on 10th Street anymore and neither is Jules Loeb.

You're right, we said, the store is out on McHenry, and Jules' sons, Stan and Lloyd, are continuing the same type of operation.

Then we have the House of Carpets with Jeff Cowan, the Watson Bros. Upholstery and Salas Bros., as well as Franklin & Downs funeral homes.

And don't forget the daddy of them all — the E & J Gallo Winery.

Modesto may not have a center at the moment, we said, but it still has a heart.

Wink yawned and went back to sleep.

—*February 26, 1994*

MODESTO ON MY MIND

Part V — Folk Tales:
How the Flatlanders survive under the sun

No noise is good noise

WHATEVER BECAME OF MODESTO'S anti-noise ordinance? Or anybody else's for that matter. There are several possible answers.

1. It was lost in the din.
2. It never got a hearing.
3. The appeal fell on deaf ears.

It is true that we have come to live with a high level of background noise as part of the environment with much less concern than has been shown for other assaults on the senses — the visual pollution caused by littering, for example.

Without regard to its effectiveness, at least there is a continuing effort to discourage and reduce littering. Offenders are even occasionally fined.

But when did you ever see a sign saying "Shh!" or "Hold It Down"? Speed limits are posted everywhere; decibel limits are nowhere to be found. Even the respectful old "Quiet — Hospital Zone" sign has disappeared, probably shattered by the electronic screech of approaching emergency vehicles.

What can we expect from a society that has machines running machines, amplifiers amplifying amplifiers, engines racing engines? The best to hope for would be a limited ceasefire, a nightly truce, and eight-hour period of R & R before the battle begins again at sunup. The background level does drop a little at night, but even in Modesto it is not all that peaceful in the country.

The high-powered drone along McHenry goes far into the night. Into the mornings on weekends. The caravans of heavy diesels rumble down the overnight freeway run between Los Angeles and San Francisco. A long freight train rattles along the mainline, chugging and wailing its way through the valley. A jet airliner whistles in for a late night landing, then roars off on the return flight.

Modesto, of course, is typical of any city its size in the matter of noise pollution. Certainly in this country. But not necessarily throughout the entire industrial world.

West Germany, for one, has had it with too much noise. Going back to 1968, the German burghers began their quiet campaign for quiet. It soon became the the country's No. 1 environmental issue. Out of that have come day and night limits on the decibel count in commercial and residential areas and they are enforced. Metal garbage cans are verboten; the plastic containers produce no 4 a.m. clang. Construction noises have been muffled and airports must close up shop at 11 p.m.

The information comes from a recent piece in the Los Angeles Times by Gunter Haaf, a scholarly reaction to his stay in this country. He is a West German science writer on a fellowship to the United States. And he intimates that he has not had a good night's sleep since he left Germany.

Having traveled the breadth of this country, he is ready to concede its undisputed leadership as the land of perpetual noise. He has failed to find any enduring silence from coast to coast — even during an overnight stay in a national park. At sunrise the park was invaded by a swarm of dune buggies.

Haaf's research led him to find this country is fully five years behind Germany in noise abatement regulation and, even then, our laws are lacking in teeth and rather loosely enforced. As an environmental issue, noise pollution remains at a low priority.

Haaf figures it will be at least another five years before we can catch up and quiet down.

There is some comfort here but not much. Because the irony is that in the meantime, we cannot even suffer in silence.

—February 5, 1977

The powerful aviation lobby

KEEPING TABS ON THE EFFECTIVE AND powerful Sacramento lobbies is really the province of Martin Smith, the McClatchy Newspapers political editor, and a capable job he does.

But Marty missed one this week. He failed to give us an

advance rundown on one of the most effective lobbies ever to swoop into Sacramento.

The lobby? None other than Modesto's Harry Sham, who must by now be just about the best known civilian aviator in California.

Sham's sensitive political instincts were aroused last month when he got a look at AB 806, a bill which would have doubled the state property tax for aircraft owners.

He spent most of the time afterwards barnstorming as many of the state's general aviation airports as he could get to. His copilot on this mission, contractor Jim Sorensen, says they must have set down at 80 or so airports, putting up anti-AB 806 posters and talking with some 150 fixed base operators.

The Sham lobby was up against no lightweight in this campaign. The bill was the brainchild of the capable and flamboyant Assemblyman Willie Brown of San Francisco, chairman of the pivotal Assembly committee.

The silver haired lobbyist knew his flying campaign had produced a flood of letters to members of the committee. But he also knew he was up against a formidable adversary. So, after sitting in the committee room for 3-1/2 hours (which may well be the longest Harry Sham has ever remained in one place), he was flabbergasted to hear the chairman suddenly announce he was withdrawing AB 806.

By way of explanation Brown said "an 85-year-old pilot sitting in the audience" had displayed his (Brown's) picture "almost on a wanted poster" in nearly every airport in the state. "He was very effective," Brown added.

For the record, the ubiquitous Sham is 77. What he had to say immediately about the gratuitous addition of eight years to his lifetime, most of it in the air, is not printable.

Later, he decided he really didn't care what Willie Brown called him "as long as he kills that (further expletives deleted) bill."

Private aircraft owners don't need to maintain a lobbyist as long as Harry Sham is around, but they would be hard put to find a more effective one — truly an advocate of the old school.

Sham has always had some kind of an office to work out of; he now hangs his hat (and he is never without one) in a modest office at the Modesto City-County Airport, the field bearing his name. He is out there bright and early nearly every day to give flight checks as the FAA inspector.

An office, yes. But Sham was never one to mess around with paper work and files and routine correspondence. Whenever he needs to have facts and figures, he seems to know where to get them and have them at hand when the time comes. They might be jotted down on the back of an envelope or a paper napkin, but he has them.

He uses the telephone widely for his contacts, but when it is something important, he is more apt to say, "I believe I better fly over and see that bird," and off he goes. The real secret of his effectiveness is person-to-person contact. He likes to talk to people, preferably over lunch or dinner or even breakfast. His monthly tab at the Sundial must have enabled the Galas Brothers to buy out the motel.

The result of all this is that Sham's call letters and his voice are widely recognized at FAA control towers and airports throughout the state.

An insider said when Brown's committee began receiving all the letters, the assemblyman asked someone where they were coming from. He was told about Harry Sham and the "almost wanted posters." To which Brown is supposed to have replied:

"Sham? Whaddya mean Sham? This guy is the real thing."

—*May 21, 1977*

Pays to advertise, Counselor

THE NEWS EARLIER THIS WEEK WAS THAT lawyers across the nation wasted no time breaking into paid print once the professional proscription was lifted.

The early ads were nothing sensational. Mostly it was institutional type copy to gain name recognition and attract new business.

Even at that, there were some indications that the spirit of competition, which had gained favorable mention in the Supreme Court's ruling, was raising its lovely head.

The indicated followup to any such national roundup is to plumb the local situation. How has the court's ruling been received and/or acted upon by members of the bar in the old home town?

Well, the gentlemen on the first floor of this enterprise who deal with such things tell us *The Bee* has been less than whelmed by any rush of the legal practitioners to advertise their wares to the 60,000 readers of this daily publication.

In our particular situation, how else but through this medium could one ever possibly keep the Martins and the Lacy-Laceys straight?

In the former case it is highly important for the public to understand that William A. Martin is part of Martin & Hutcheson, that John W. Martin is with Price, Martin & Crabtree, and that Laurence B. Martin and Laurence H. Martin make up Martin & Martin.

Likewise that Thomas A. Lacey (with an "e") complements Brunn and Lacey, Dan W. Lacy (no "e") is found with Lacy & Kanai, and Edward M. Lacy Sr. and Jr. are joined in Lacy & Lacy.

The problem of identification in these cases requires continued advertising, similar to the campaign so effectively mounted in behalf of the Goodrich blimp.

90

Ideally, the lawyers will spare the consumer from advertising shot through with whereases or two-page spreads that begin with the following: "Know all ye by these presence," "The undersigned deposes and says," " One-half off on bankruptcies." "All fees shall hereinafter be remitted in advance." No credit cards. No deposit. No return."

A few free samples are in order. The old slogan remains a tried and true technique for positive and effective association of a name with a product or service. For instance:

Ernest M. LaCoste: "Ernie the Attorney — A Shelter for the Underdog."

Warren F. Gant: "Water Wealth Contentment Health."

Frank C. Damrell Jr.: The Consumer's Best Friend — and the Governor's, too."

George W. Kell: "The Laetrile Lawyer."

Charles E. Aguilar: "Se Habla Espanol."

Francis R. Ruggieri — Building a Better Tomorrow; Tomorrow, a Better Building."

Michael Ward: "The Way You Wear Your Hair."

L.M.(Bud) Gianelli: "Let Me Mind Your Own Business."

There is absolutely no charge for any of these, but one or two may be in use elsewhere.

There are two conspicuous omissions from the list but not because both are relatively new to the ranks of practicing attorneys. Steve Ringhoff and Don Sutton. Both of them put in many a day and night here at *The Bee* fighting deadlines and making corrections. Both of them, in fact, worked here the entire time they were putting themselves through law school.

But did either of them come rushing back here to place an ad? Ha! How soon we forget! Especially Steve. We all know that upon his departure one of our most talented artists prepared a quarter-page ad layout for him as a going-away gift. All it would take now is a little cleaning up and an insertion order.

And what do we get? Not a line from either one of them.

That's what an education will do for you.

—*July 9, 1977*

Our grapes have tender wines

A LABOR OF LOVE IN THE HANDS OF A perfectionist will surely yield a thing of beauty. There is no other way to account for the recently published work, "The Great Wine Grapes & the Wines They Make" by Bern C. Ramey.

It is a precisely, even technically, written encyclopedia of the classic wine grapes selected with authority on the simple premise that behind every great wine is a great grape.

It thus becomes the definitive catalog needed for the understanding and furtherance of the reliable and increasingly popular practice of labeling wines according to the classic variety from which they are predominantly made.

Varietal nomenclature was born in California less than 50 years ago and now has spread to wine growing regions in Australia and some of Europe, including even parts of France.

Beyond the rich depth of history and description of characteristics, cultivation and regional cultures for each of the 30 varieties selected, this magnificent, atlas-sized volume is, like the great wines it celebrates, a joy to the eye and a pleasure to the taste.

Each variety is beautifully illustrated in an unretouched full-page color photograph. Specimens meticulously selected over a three-year period at the University of California at Davis show off the cluster, leaves and berries of each variety at the peak of maturity. Equal loving care has been given to other design elements featuring a handsomely calligraphed text pleasingly framed in generous margins of white space.

The book speaks for itself. The author also does quite a bit of speaking around the world himself. He is a graduate of UC Davis, a charter member of the American Society of Enologists and a lifetime member of the International Wine and Food Society. He now lives in San Francisco and is a vice president of Browne Vintners, the wine division of Joseph E. Seagrams & Sons, Inc.

And believe me, he is a perfectionist. We grew up together through our salad years on the shores of Lake Erie in the valley of murky Maumee, Toledo, Ohio. Bern may the only true Renaissance man I know. He was an avid reader, with wide and consuming interests, a classical scholar, an accomplished musician with an urge to excel at everything he tries. I took him a couple of times at mumblety-peg and occasionally, when the forehand smash was working (which wasn't often),in ping-pong.

And it looks as if Bern passed some of that along. The exquisite photography for "Great Grapes" was done by his son, Timothy, a Chicago-based professional whose work shows that same streak of perfectionism.

As if the book were not classy enough, it carries a forward by Maynard A. Amerine, professor of enology emeritus at UC Davis, one of the world's foremost wine authorities, and certainly the father of California's excellence in the field. Bern studied under Prof. Amerine. and over the years they became close friends.

"But he still treats me like a student," Bern confided. He had finished the first draft of the text for one variety and took it in for his mentor to look over. Amerine went to work on it as though he were correcting a term paper. Then he looked up and slowly shook his head. Bern knew what was coming.

"Too many Rameyisms?" Amerine nodded. That was his word for Bern's flair for spicing his writing and speaking with finely turned phrases. They are entertaining, they give relief, and he does it well. But for Amerine they were signs of sloth and imprecision.

"There are good writers and there are lazy writers," he told his pupil, "but there is no such thing as a good lazy writer. Now get to work."

Bern obviously did. Still, he managed to slip in a few delightful Rameyisms — like his characterization of the Sylvaner variety as a "thick-skinned old cuss from Austria."

For me, however, "Great Grapes" pleasantly confirmed two things my tired and uneducated old palate has been trying to tell me for lo! these many years.

1. "Chardonnay (is) California's finest white, if not finest wine."

2. "Cabernet Sauvignon — one of the world's and certainly America's greatest red wine variety."

I'll clink to that.

—*July 29, 1978*

The mystery of Modesto

JUST WHEN WE WERE GETTING LESS PARANOID about snide references to Modesto, just when we were basking in the doldrums of summer, confident that our Bay Area antagonists had gone dormant, we were hit from an unexpected quarter.

The *New York Review of Books*, which is to the literary-intellectual world what the *Wall Street Journal* is to the business community, has become the medium in this insidious campaign.

One entertaining feature of the *NY Review* is its personals column — want ads that cry out with the yearning of lonely souls in search of kindred spirits, but — we hasten to add — on a less earthy and much loftier plane than similar columns in the underground press like, say, the *Berkeley Barb*.

There it was for all to see nestled in among the personals on page 70 of the Sept. 27 *New York Review.*

Five attractive Bay Area women seek the following male companionship: one mature humanist; one ambitious, organized Armenian gourmet jock; one Jewish Pynchon fan with good legs; one Swedish Christian intellectual; one self-conscious, slightly neurotic, unsophisticated poor dancer desiring fulfilling relationship. P.O. Box 4892, Modesto, CA 95352.

First, any potential respondent of this appeal would have to decide whether it is a genuine search for soulmates or rather some elaborate spoof designed to titillate the esoteric tastes of the *New York Review's* elitist readership.

There is a good deal of evidence to support the latter conclusion.

In the first place, what could five women with such widely divergent definitions of Mr. Right possibly have in common that would bring them together for any purpose? This is difficult to imagine even after making liberal allowances for the Bay Area association, a residence factor which does lend some flickering credence to the possibility of a sincere appeal.

There is a much more basic question, however, which casts strong doubt on the sincerity of the ad. Why would five such women, who have already demonstrated a degree of sophistication by using a Modesto post office box, turn to the select national circulation of the *New York Review* when their order could be readily filled from within the reach of the greater Modesto area?

A couple of them could be a trifle troublesome. We're a little low on mature humanists at the moment, and the Jewish Pynchon fan might take some digging, especially if the good legs are essential.

The others are all in good supply. Turlock, for instance, abounds in Swedish Christian intellectuals, and the newspaper business itself is awash with self-conscious, slightly neurotic, unsophisticated poor dancers.

Anyone, even a Bay Arean, who has ever found her way to Modesto's main post office would automatically know these things.

There is, of course, the possibility that the whole thing is not a spoof at all, but a carefully coded message of the kind inserted by spies or lovers. It could say nothing more than "I'm thinking of you on this day, honey, and don't forget to let the cat out." On the other hand, the message may be coming out of an unscrambler at this very moment in the underground cipher room of a foreign intelligence agency: "Overthrow plan must be delayed; governor returned to state unexpectedly."

The possibility of authenticity cannot be entirely discounted, however. One strong bit of evidence is the return address. The post office box number is genuine and the ZIP code is right.

Moreover, anyone who understands the psychology of personal ad-writing will recognize the zinger in this one.

A good, productive ad has to attract attention. After all, it is competing with scores of others. You can't get by just with Armenian gourmets or Swedish intellectuals. The ad must jump out.

And that, of course, accounts for the Modesto return address. A Modesto return address in the *New York Review of Books*! A stroke of genius. Think of the interest that will attract, the mystery and fascination it will create. The replies will come pouring in. Probably are already.

Nor does it end there. When the time comes to answer all the promising nibbles, think how the suspense will be heightened for some mature New Jersey humanist when this response to the mystery of Modesto brings return mail from Stockton.

A stroke of pure genius.

—*September 8, 1979*

Gone is the luster

EVERYBODY LOVES A MYSTERY, THEY SAY, although we are beginning to harbor doubts. The old saying may be nothing more than a slogan promoted by the association of whodunit writers.

In this space last week we sought to explore the mystery of a rather intriguing ad which appeared in the personals column of the Sept. 17 *New York Review of Books.*

As you may remember the ad purported to come from "five attractive Bay Area women" with specifications that read like the list for a Berkeley scavenger hunt.

Specifically, they were looking for "one mature humanist; one ambitious, organized Armenian gourmet jock; one Jewish Pynchon fan with good legs; one Swedish Christian intellectual and one self-conscious, slightly neurotic unsophisticated poor dancer desiring a fulfilling relationship."

Taken in context with other ads appearing in the *New York Review's* personals column, this one in itself was not particularly remarkable. What distinguished it and piqued the curiosity was that replies were directed to a Modesto post office box.

The replies, we can assure you, have been prompt. And the Modesto boxholders, we can also assure you, are not amused. The letters in response began arriving late last week to the utter bewilderment of the boxholders, who had absolutely no clue to the source of the letters until we took pains to publicize the mysterious message.

There was one quick stab of concern that in so doing we had erred in reproducing the box number. It was quickly allayed. Replies had started coming before then and are continuing to arrive from all parts of the country, far beyond our reach.

None of these considerations is of any solace to the boxholders, who understandably feel put upon as the innocent victims of a misdirected prank.

More than that, they are shocked and appalled at the content of the mail they are receiving. "You wouldn't believe the things these people are writing," they said, "and many of these are supposedly respectable people like doctors and lawyers and other professional men."

This would tend to dilute last week's assessment of the *New York Review's* readership, which we thought was generally more refined than that of its second cousins in the underground press like, for instance, the *Berkeley Barb*.

The post office could be of little assistance. It is required by law to put the mail in the box to which it is addressed. If the wrong number is inadvertently used, there is no way of knowing that until someone complains.

The boxholders totally reject the idea that anyone of their acquaintance is playing a prank on them, certainly not this kind of prank. "We don't even know people like that," they said, "even remotely." They could change their number, but they prefer not to. Their immediate concern is to confine the damage.

The quickest way was to put in a telephone call to the *New York Review's* advertising department to find out whether the published number was a mistake and also to make sure it would be changed if the ad was scheduled to run in subsequent issues of the *Review*.

The published box number turned out to be the one furnished by the advertiser, but the ad is not scheduled to appear again. Once satisfied that the wrong box number was furnished, the *Review* will contact the advertiser and attempt to find out what happened.

All of which serves to take the sheen off a mystery which only last week glistened with fascination and promise.

And the stroke of pure genius turned into a foul ball.

—September 15, 1979

All straightened out

NO MATTER WHAT THE MAN SAYS, IT was too good to pass up. He had his needle out for what he called the *New York Review of Books* fiasco.

You run across some nutty ad in that egghead magazine, he says, and just because it has a Modesto reference, you have to make a big thing out of it and look what happens.

He's talking about the classified ad in the Sept. 27 *New York Review* purporting to come from "five attractive Bay Area women" in search of some rather interesting male companionship.

Not an unusual ad for the personals column of that magazine, but the man was right. We were taken by the cosmopolitan tastes expressed in the ad. Specifically, these women were looking for "one mature humanist; one ambitious, organized Armenian gourmet jock; one Jewish Pynchon fan with good legs; one Swedish Christian intellectual and one self-conscious, slightly neurotic, unsophisticated poor dancer desiring a fulfilling relationship."

Obviously, the man said, the whole thing was the work of some kook. And just because the return address is a Modesto post office box, you have to hype it up into some kind of a big mystery. Then see what happens. The post office box turns out to belong some innocent people who all of a sudden start getting all this raunchy mail from all over the country and don't know what hit them. At least, they don't know until you make a big deal out of it. And all the time some kook is sitting out there laughing at their expense and at yours. Right?

Wrong. We now have good reason to believe the ad was genuine. The only thing wrong about it was the P.O. box number — and that was unintentional.

Whereupon we produced for the man a typewritten letter received last month and signed "The Modesto Five."

"Well, at least you have solved one mystery," the letter says. "We now know why we haven't received any letters. The P.O. box number was in error for the ad we placed. It had two digits transposed. We apologize to all those that have been inconvenienced by our mail. Perhaps those letters could be returned to the post office and placed in the proper box. After all, we are for real and so was the ad, so please write."

So you're doing it again, the man said. How do you know that letter is for real? How do you know that P.O. box number is any better than the first one?

Whereupon we produced another letter, received one week later, from Kathy Metzger of the *New York Review's* advertising department.

"I received a letter today from the woman who originally

placed the classified ad beginning 'five attractive Bay Area women'. She had transposed two numbers in her box number when she sent me this ad. Her correct number is 4982. The ad will be repeated in our November 8 issue with the correct number.

"I have sent a letter today to the holder of the other box number explaining the situation. Thank you for calling the problem to my attention."

Now, then, that settles that, let us hope. However, there is little likelihood that the Modesto five will get any of the mail that was attracted by their first ad. The boxholders who received it, as we said, were not amused. And, although they can accept the explanation of the mixup and can now laugh about it, they saw no reason to preserve the kind of mail they were getting.

The man was still not convinced.

They advertised themselves as "five attractive Bay Area women," he said, but this letter is signed "The Modesto Five." How do you know what they are?

Doesn't matter. They could be one or the other or both or neither. The one thing we do know with reasonable certainty is that their letter came from Modesto. It was postmarked Stockton.

—*October 6, 1979*

Good humor and bad

THE TIMES ARE MEAN AND THE CITY IS playing hardball. First it was the crackdown on World Series pools, and now it's the crusade to silence Good Humor Men.

You know, Good Humor Men — or perhaps in these touchy times, Good Humor Persons. You must have read where the police

101

cited eight of these affable ice cream vendors last summer as they plied their trade through the neighborhoods, sounding their familiar chimes.

It's against the law, the officers said. The Modesto Municipal Code contains a provision of 20 years' standing against the use of amplified sound for commercial advertising on any city street or public place. Not altogether a bad law, you understand but, like any law, subject to reasonable interpretation.

At first, the Good Humor People, true to their dispositions, just laughed. But when the officers wrote out citations, they turned off their chimes, wiped off their smiles and learned how to frown. There are, after all, limits to the extent of Good Humorism.

Are those chimes really advertising? asked Happy. There's no vocal pitch, Jolly reminded him. The chimes are just a theme song, Jolly pouted. A theme song! That's it, Happy said, his good humor returning. So that makes the chimes entertainment, not advertising. They decided to go to court.

Fortune was on their side. Obviously sitting on the august panel of municipal court jurors were many whose childhood was not so long gone but that they could recall the joyous tinkle of those chimes with all their promise of frozen goodies on a hot summer's afternoon.

Not advertising at all, said the jury. Nothing but a harmless tradition. Case dismissed.

Well, yes and no. A harmless tradition, certainly. Think back when street vendors of one kind or another were much more common. The challenge for them was to come up with a distinctive sound so the housewife could tell who was coming down the street without looking.

The produce hucksters leaned heavily on bells and gongs. Some of them, especially the Italians, sang out lustily in a call that was all their own. The popcorn wagon had a shrill steam whistle. The surly ash men, who were nevertheless very important in the days of coal furnaces, blew a raucous single note out of a battered tin horn. The rag pickers and junk men relied on their own voices, but each also developed a distinctive call. The scissors grinders came along only about twice a year but there was no mistaking them. They used a two-toned bell that give off a sharp, penetrating cling-clang.

The tradition is there, all right, but as for case dismissed, that is another matter. This case has been decided, the city says, but the law is still on the books and will continue to be enforced with citations. A hollow victory, after all.

But be of good cheer, Good Humor People, for we have a plan. The solution to this oppression lies in the code itself, and the key word is "amplified." The prohibition is against amplified sound. All you have to do is get rid of those canned chimes and go back to the real thing in the tradition of your predecessors. Given the ambient decibel level of today, you may have to install rather large chimes or rig up a resonating box, but those are mere details.

Will it work? Of course it will. How do you think the Salvation Army Santa Clauses have managed to keep from getting busted every time Christmas rolls around?

—*November 3, 1979*

The mayor stands up

WE SAW A LITTLE DIFFERENT SIDE of the mayor the other night when Peggy Mensinger availed herself of the opportunity to address the City Council.

103

Speaking to the council is nothing new for the mayor, of course, but this occasion was special. She was speaking from the public podium, having turned over the gavel to the vice mayor, as she has in every instance since 1978 whenever there has been any discussion or action on the community center.

The mayor took herself out of these deliberations after determining that she had a possible conflict of interest. It was the kind of circumspection that is characteristic of her performance as a public office-holder. Her family owns property across the street from the community center site — specifically, the American Lumber Co.

That wasn't quite enough for the group that is now challenging the city's plans to start work on the first phase of the downtown redevelopment project. They say that having acknowledged such a possible conflict, it was not proper for the mayor to have appointed the council's three-member Special Projects Committee, which developed and recommended the present project. The committee's recommendation was subsequently approved by five of the six sitting members of the council.

The questioning of the propriety of the routine designation of the committee members was just a little more than the mayor could take, especially when, in fact, it involved only council members who had volunteered for the assignment.

Mayor Mensinger took the public podium and began by thanking the council for the opportunity "to appear before this distinguished body." It was the last trace of a smile we saw on her face. It was also the first time we noticed that her eyes occasionally flash when she speaks, as she rarely has, in defense of her own performance.

In denouncing what she called this "media mayhem," she took a swipe at us, too.

She said it was bad enough "to watch a television screen while a man standing on a street corner makes allegations aimed at destroying the reputation for integrity you and your husband have spent a lifetime establishing." But even more frustrating, she said, "is having the newspaper in your own city day after day repeating the charges while failing to use 95 percent of the background material you have supplied in response."

Well, good for the mayor, we say. We acknowledge that coverage of the kind of controversy now swirling around the city center project, along with the published viewpoints of various proponents and opponents and letters to the editor, tends to get repetitive and can become a difficult endurance test even for those with the thickest of skins.

We also admit that we may have been remiss here in not rising sooner to the defense of the mayor's record. If that is the case, however, it is an oversight into which we were lulled by the belief that Mayor Mensinger's record in this area needed no defense.

Nobody on this council or any other one has been more attentive to the ethics of public office. She has been an active member of Common Cause from the beginning and a champion of everything it stands for — fair political practices and full disclosure of financial support. In her own campaigns she has limited individual contributions to $25.

Mayor Mensinger concluded by offering to match "my record in Modesto and my motives against those of any of my critics, especially the real forces behind this incredible campaign of media mayhem."

It would be no contest. Her hours of voluntary civic service are unmatched and her dedication to the demands of public office has been unswerving. Even her interest in meeting the need for a community center predates her election to office.

105

It was her efforts, as chairman of a council-appointed citizen's committee in 1968, which ultimately persuaded the council to purchase the old Lincoln school property and set it aside as the future site of a community center.

The possibilities of the Lincoln site, which were limited to begin with, were further diminished by the subsequent construction of the Ralston Tower. In a way, it is ironic that Peggy Mensinger, who worked so hard for a community center before she was in office, would have to disqualify herself in that effort after she was in office because another site was chosen.

But the city's ownership of the Lincoln site, which now figures in the redevelopment area along with the present site, has helped to keep the community center idea alive.

—August 4, 1984

Land of Lincoln

IT'S HARD TO BELIEVE THAT THE OLD Lincoln School site some day will become something other than the old Lincoln School site.

It has been sitting there rather forlornly for 16 years now, waiting for something to develop. In the meantime, it has served as a partially paved over parking lot, a staging area for the courthouse bus shuttle and a productive summer vegetable garden for some of our green thumbs.

The Board of Education tore down the old Lincoln School in 1964 and replaced it with relocatable classrooms. After five years the board decided there were just not enough kids left in the old downtown neighborhoods and sold the site to the city in 1970. The city gradually acquired the rest of the property in the block, which included a church and a couple of homes.

The hopes were high for the site in those days. Not long after the property was cleared, a sign went up designating it as the site of Modesto's future community center. And all sorts of tentative plans were discussed. There was to be a little theater and a big auditorium. There was even one suggestion to close off I Street and extend the site into the triangle where Ralston Tower now stands.

At the time, St. Paul's Episcopal Church was located on that corner in a nice old edifice and the rest was the little park that now provides the setting for the tower. Many objected to the idea of losing the little church, but it was outgrowing the building anyway, and a bigger stumbling block was probably the idea of closing off I Street.

In any case, a number of things happened to delay or change the plans, not the least of which was financing. Then, Ralston Tower came along and just about everybody is happy with the way that turned out. Finally, in the late '70s, the City Council decided the so-called Sears site would be a better location for a downtown community center, and we all know what has happened since then.

Now, what do we do with the old Lincoln School site? Another Ralston Tower was favored at one time, but the same kind of financing isn't easy to find anymore. City Hospital once thought it might like to expand onto the property but has since changed its plans. An office building or a shopping center also figured in the informal discussion.

So the old Lincoln School site is just sitting there — but not for long.

The council canvassed several hundred developers to find out what kind of interest there was and what sort of development would be best suited to the location. Eventually the council decided that, from a redevelopment point of view, a nice little neighborhood shopping center would make the best use of the five-acre site.

In casting around, the council members became impressed with the work of Westar Associates, a Costa Mesa development firm which specializes in just such centers, having built a number of them on sites ranging from five to 20 acres. The council picked Westar to pursue the project.

Enter Peter Koetting. Not only was he an executive vice president of Westar, but he grew up in Modesto. He remembers when you could buy groceries downtown, when Lucky was at 10th and L, and Justesen's was at 14th and J and McHenry Village was out in the country.

He has jumped into the project with energy and enthusiasm. He thinks it is an ideal location for an area that is not now served. He has signed up Save Mart to anchor the center and foresees no problem leasing other retail space, including a restaurant. He has found public favor for the idea, especially from the people in Ralston Tower.

What he does not quite understand is that the City Council, having decided on a shopping center for the site, now seems to be hesitant about going ahead with it — even though it has obtained the usual 4-2 vote of approval.

All we can offer in that respect is that he probably has been away from Modesto too long.

Whatever the case, he shouldn't have any trouble finding a suitable name. We know developers always prefer names that end with Place or Plaza or Center. But after he has gone through all of those, there's always one he can fall back on.

He can call it The Old Lincoln School Site.

—December 20, 1986

Losing our assets

LET'S SEE. WE LOST THE COUNTY FAIR and the state university to Turlock. Stockton took our postmark. The super-collider went to Texas. And the Chamber of Commerce is not enthusiastic about going after a UC campus here.

If that's not enough, we are about to lose another institution. Ross Wurm and Associates, our premier public relations firm, will hang it up after 30 years in the business.

Ross himself will leave Dec. 17 to retire in Olympia, Wash., and Dorothy Mortensen, his partner for all these years, will close the office at the end of the year. And with that will go one of the most creative and effective advocates for California agriculture in the nation.

Ross grew up in Oregon and after coming out of World War II, kicked around the country, working on newspapers and gravitating toward farm publications. He never quite knew what he really wanted to do until he went into advertising in Chicago. That's when he realized that advertising was most of all the one thing he wanted to do.

Finally, it dawned on him that he knew quite a bit about farming, and he would make a good agricultural P.R. man. He was right about that. First of all, he is an excellent writer, and he is strong on research. If he is going to beat the drums about something, he wants to know everything there is to know about it. And he does. Plus the fact that he is one of the most gregarious people around, a great story-teller with an irrepressible irreverence for just about everything.

Since he was going to specialize in agriculture, he decided to go where the action was — right here. Along the way, he has snagged some good accounts. Tri/Valley Growers, Dow Chemical, the tomato growers and who knows what other agricultural interests.

We first became aware of Ross Wurm in the late '50s or early '60s — whenever the nation went through the Great Cranberry Scare. Some of the Eastern bogs had been sprayed with a pesticide, and the story started going around just before Thanksgiving time that cranberries weren't safe to eat. Sales plummeted and growers were going broke. In the middle of all the hysteria, Ross staged a cranberry cocktail party to restore confidence in the seasonal berry. Whether it did or not, we don't know, but the Associated Press picked up the story and distributed it nationwide.

Ross also created the Okra Festival long before Cajun food became the rave because he felt the much maligned gumbo pods needed recognition. And he had a hand in last year's Pig's Feet Festival at the Westley Hotel.

He occasionally took on political campaigns, although we always had the feeling he was a little picky about this. He had to like the client before he would handle the campaign. One of his early clients was Richard Lyng, who decided he'd like to give up his Modesto seed business and get into government. He ran for the State Senate. He didn't make that, but he is now the U.S. Secretary of Agriculture. Ross figured that was a better job anyway.

His most recent political client was Balvino Irizarry, who was elected to the Modesto City Council last year. Ross liked his style, and said it was the first time he had a client whose name looked like an eye chart.

We thought maybe we should check some of this information in the files. That's when we came across the biographical form which had been submitted by Ross in 1972. The first page looks pretty routine — name, address, date of birth, etc. But from there on it is pure, vintage Ross Wurm. Here a sample of his answers:

Details of your occupation, profession or business career, various positions held and date: 1958 to date, a public relations practitioner and counselor; 1950 to 1958, vendor of horse collars, snaps, rings, hames and other tack and gear; 1950-1954, cow milker, Bellflower, Calif.; 1946-50, took correspondence course in newspaper writing, worked as copy boy on Walla Walla, Wash. Bulletin; 1941-45, assisted Gen. Patton in winning WWII.

If you have ever held public office, please give the name or names of the offices and date of service: Was once an accredited baseball scorer, 1945-47.

Church affiliation: Former member of the congregation of the Sons and Daughters of I Will Arise.

Outline any athletic interests: Collect used athletic supporters. When dyed and provided with knit covering they make excellent nest for Baltimore Orioles or night jars.

Any additional information: Currently have 400-page manuscript on autobiography. Will forward after typing.

Wonder if he is done with that yet?

—December 10, 1988

Commuters Anonymous

THE VOICE ON THE PHONE WAS pleasant and cordial. The man preferred not to give his name. He was calling out of curiosity.

"I am one of the hated commuters," he said. I drive 140 miles to work and back every day, five days a week. My wife is a commuter, too. She drives 60 miles round trip daily. And what we'd like to know is what you have against commuters."

There was a pause while we tried to think of the best way to convince this man that we are really not anti-commuter. We couldn't say some of our best friends are commuters because it's not true.

He didn't wait. "We keep hearing about all the commuters coming here, pushing up the price of housing, filling up the farm land, crowding the schools and clogging traffic.

"We're here because we like it here. We have two kids in school, and we want to put down roots. We go to as many of the school things and parent meetings as we can, but we don't have much time. It's no picnic driving all those miles every day. We both have good jobs, but we'd give them up in a minute if we could find anything comparable here. But we can't. So we have to live here and work there. And it still takes two paychecks to keep up. Is that so awful?"

We said no, it wasn't awful. In fact, we have to have a certain amount of respect for anyone who will make that kind of sacrifice — every day — to live here.

"We figure we can do better by the kids this way," he said, "than what we could afford to do by living closer to work."

We told him our reaction was not really one of hostility to commuters, but rather of shock that they were able to find us.

Oh, we've always had a few Bay Area commuters around — some airline pilots, some firemen and some others who had flexible schedules and didn't have to make the trip quite every day.

But we never dreamed the time would come when people would start streaming over the Altamont, negotiating the Manteca bypass and finding their way down here through our outer defenses. Not this soon, anyway.

"You mentioned the Manteca bypass," he said. "Instead of figuring out new ways to sock it to the commuter, you ought to be out crusading to get that thing fixed. People are getting killed in that trap."

We agreed that traffic safety demands the highest priority for the Manteca bypass. In fact, we told him that thing was obsolete before it got off the drawing boards.

What got the Manteca bypass started was weekend traffic, not daily traffic. People from the Bay Area heading back and forth to the mountains for skiing or summer recreation. They so clogged the streets that Mantecans would get out on weekends with petitions, getting signatures from drivers tied up in traffic.

By the time Caltrans got ready to build it, funds for highways were just about dried up. So they did it on the cheap. But it has to be fixed.

Now Caltrans says commuter traffic all over the state has grown so heavy that they will never be able to build enough highways even if they had the money. Other measures will have to be taken. The chief culprit is one man, one car. It's going to take more car pooling, mass transportation and staggered work schedules.

So, what's in the future? The *Wall Street Journal* had a story this week saying that business and industry are discovering the Central Valley and are inclined to move in here rather than expand or build new plants in major metropolitan areas for the same reasons commuters are coming — cheaper land, cheaper housing, less congestion.

And what does that mean? Well, it means that what we see happening in the Livermore-Pleasanton-Dublin area will be happening all over again right here. Land and housing prices will go up and congestion will increase.

In the long run it means that if the jobs come here, commuters will be coming in here, as well as going out.

Maybe even coming in from the Bay Area.

—February 18, 1989

113

One at a time

ONE OF THE THINGS IT'S GETTING HARD to do around here is find a store where you can buy one — just one — of anything.

We mean things like soap and paper towels and cotter keys and washers.

With soap, you buy three and get one free. It says so right on the package, and they're all sealed together as tight as a drum.

Paper towels come at least two rolls to a package, but the featured package contains a year's supply.

Cotter keys? Nobody ever wants just one, so you get nine in a package. And washers. There's 22 of them in that little plastic box, even though you'll never need another one in your lifetime.

Hardware is probably the toughest thing to find in the "one of" department. Everybody handles hardware these days — drug stores, supermarkets, variety stores, gift shops, nurseries, etc.

But they have the same things. Little boxes of nails, packages of assorted screws, cup hooks, shelf brackets and picture hangers.

It makes us old timers weep for the day Turner Hardware went out of business. Turner's was one of Modesto's venerable pioneer businesses, about the same vintage as the Modesto Lumber Co., whose fate now also is uncertain.

Turner's main store was located at 9th and H Streets in the building which has since been remodeled and revitalized by Mid-Valley Engineering.

At Turner's you could buy anything from a hame to a horse collar, and you could get just one of them.

One time we needed a little coupling that had fine female threads on one end and coarse male threads on the other. It was used to extend the rod that goes from the plunger to the drain stopper in a bathroom wash basin.

114

We took it down to Turner's and showed it to the man and he knew what it was right away.

That's also something that's hard to find these days.

He allowed as how he had some of those and headed for a wall full of bins. He rummaged around for a while, couldn't find it but said he was still pretty sure they had one. He disappeared down the basement steps and pretty soon reappeared with exactly what we were looking for — and just one of them.

On another occasion, when the man had to check the basement for an item, we were bold enough to follow him down, just to get at look at it.

It was as if somebody had laid in a huge supply of everything anybody would need for the next 200 years.

It was a whole other world of hardware down there, with boxes and bins and barrels and crates. Things hanging from the ceiling, peeking out from shelves and nesting in tall stacks from the floor. We're sure we saw some parts left over from the horse and buggy days.

The sad fact is that nobody seems to want to buy one of anything anymore. They're going the other way. They want to get everything in wholesale quantities.

Stores that are doing the business are these no-frills warehouse-type operations with merchandise stacked up to the ceiling.

You go into these places and you have to be careful not to get run over by hot rod fork-lift drivers, who skitter around like water bugs, or rammed by somebody pushing a cart the size of a pickup truck. These monster carts are loaded with cases of soft drinks, drums of washing powder, 33-gallon bags of pretzels and enough dog food for 101 Dalmatians.

We often wondered what people did with all this stuff until we saw one customer with a boxed storage shed on his cart. He acquired the shed to keep all the stuff he bought and will probably need another one before long.

All this is bound to have had some effect on the retailing market, and we have only to look at what is happening to department stores to get an idea. They're having tough times.

Otherwise, here in California, as the June election approaches, there remains one thing we can reasonably be assured, and perhaps grateful, we'll always be able to get just one of:

Jerry Brown.

—May 16, 1992

'He was a good guy'

THE SUDDEN DEATH OF JULIO GALLO last week in a Jeep accident hit this community like a ton of bricks. Never have we heard so many sincere expressions of sorrow and sympathy, not only from the few who knew him well, but from those who knew the name, maybe a little about the family and about the empire he had spent a lifetime helping create.

People felt genuine loss because they admired this man — the way he lived, his dedication to the work and the enjoyment he got from it, his devotion to family and the way he treated those who worked for him.

It was more than just adulation of someone rich and famous. Beyond the fame and fortune, perhaps in spite of it, people perceived Julio Gallo as a nice guy, a gentle man who treated people like human beings.

Naturally, this story brought out the media all over the world. We heard sound bites from every wine expert, real or imagined, throughout the state. Some, on the basis of one or two phone conversations or perhaps a meeting with Julio Gallo, felt qualified to tell us with authority what all this would mean to the future of the winery.

Baloney. These people probably know less about the family or the workings of the winery than either you or we do. But they don't hesitate to give full and authoritative reactions.

One of the most sensible responses came from a professor of enology at the famed UC Davis graduate school. Sorry we missed the name. It wasn't our own Maynard Amerine, a professor emeritus there, who is regarded by many as the father of California's wine industry. But the response was much the same as he would have offered.

The interviewer, who was trying to ask hard questions perhaps derived from the recent book on the Gallo family, wanted to know about Julio's role in the early days when the winery made mostly inexpensive wines and some that were fortified.

The professor cut her down to size. That was then, he said, when America was not really a wine-drinking country. Those in the wine business had to produce the wines people would drink — sweet wines, the ports and sherries and the cheap jug wines. The Gallos did, too. But all the time they were also bending every effort to improve things, to educate growers and consumers to a taste for higher quality.

They produced some excellent, still inexpensive table wines, then they went to some outstanding varietals and to brandy, and now they are getting ready to market some estate bottled wine.

All in all, the Gallos have done more to raise the standard of wine-making and to educate the palates of wine drinkers in this country than any other force.

Somebody who knew Julio Gallo well was the late Harry

Sham, long-time manager of the Modesto City-County Airport.

Harry liked to take people on tours in his airplane, where he was known in every control tower from Crescent City to San Diego.

Getting Julio into his airplane wasn't that easy, so he persuaded him to take a boat trip through the Delta.

In the course of this trip, Harry had the boat pull into a small island that had a very lively bar and restaurant, frequented mostly by Delta ranch hands and a few yachtsmen who knew about it.

The ebullient owner served as maitre de, bartender and master of ceremonies. When he saw Harry come in he rushed over to give him a bear hug. Harry introduced him to Julio. The owner called him Julius, put his arm around him and said, "Oh, yeah, I know Julius. I see him all the time on the TV, riding around the vineyard on his horse and singing 'Jimmy Cracked Corn'." He was alluding to a Gallo commercial that was airing in those days.

Harry said Julio roared. He liked the owner, liked the place and enjoyed the people. And he wasn't the least bit disturbed that a good many of them were drinking Gallo wine.

Many times, Harry said, Julio told him how much he enjoyed himself that afternoon in the Delta.

We knew Harry well enough to know what he would have said about Julio Gallo's death.

He would have echoed what we have heard so often from men and women around town.

"He was a good guy."

—May 8, 1993

118

The Gallo know-how

WHEN THE E&J GALLO WINERY decided it would take a step up and get into the varietal wine market, there wasn't a great deal of consternation among the many producers of premium wines.

They were rather lulled into complacency by the connoisseurs and all the snooty wine critics who said simply that the Gallos would not make it in that field. The Gallo name, they said, was inextricably bound to jug wines and other cheap wines. They never could make it in the varietal field.

That didn't daunt Ernest Gallo, the marketing genius of this duo, or the late Julio Gallo, the winemaker who knew what he wanted, and he knew how to get it.

Long before the Gallos went into the production of varietals, they began a program of encouraging growers in the San Joaquin Valley who supplied much of their grapes to redo their vineyards. They urged them to pull out their old Thompson seedless grapes, which were the basis for many of the cheap wines, and plant varietals. And they provided a financial incentive. The grapes included a cabernet sauvignon, a zinfandel, a chardonnay and a sauvignon blanc. And, of course, they did the same thing with their own vineyards.

Within a few years, when they were satisfied that there was an ample supply of the grapes they needed to begin producing these wines on a Gallo scale, they went into the field and came out with excellent varietals selling for about $7 a bottle — a very reasonable price for a wine of that quality.

In a relatively short time they became the leading producer of varietal wines. You have to know the Gallos have arrived in the varietal field when Frank J. Prial, the *New York Times* wine writer, travels to Modesto to find out how the Gallos do this and what they are up to.

"Today we are the largest supplier of varietals in the business," Ernest Gallo told him, and he showed him a report from a San Francisco consultant estimating that Gallo is already 50 percent larger than the next largest varietal producer and is continuing to widen the gap.

In his Sept. 15 article, Prial is most interested in the recent step up in the varietal field — high quality wines from their own estates. This is known in the trade as "estate bottled," and it means all the wine comes from grapes grown in the winery's vineyards.

For this purpose, the Gallos acquired about 4,000 acres of land in the Dry Creek region of northern Sonoma County, where they could develop the vineyard and nurture the grapes to their own meticulous standards.

Estate bottled wine is usually considered the top of the line and is pricey, both because of the attention given to the grapes and the fact that the vintage is limited.

Gallo recently came out with its first entry in the estate bottled market — A 1991 chardonnay that sells for $30 a bottle. There were only 3,250 cases made, a very small amount by Gallo standards.

Prial notes that the chardonnay has been favorably received by critics and he finds it "in the classic California style. It breaks no new ground but can easily hold its own against most of America's best chardonnays. It's well structured, full and rich. . ."

Noting that the wine has come to the market ready to drink, he quotes Ernest Gallo as saying, "Making a wine ready to drink is my responsibility, not the consumer's."

That helps to explain why the the second entry in the estate bottled market, a cabernet sauvignon to be priced at about $60, was held off at Ernest Gallo's insistence. He didn't think it was ready.

That sounds more like it would have been a decision of Julio Gallo, who made the final blending of the estate-bottled chardonnay, then sadly was killed in a May 2 automobile accident before his pride and joy reached the marketplace.

Prial comments on the elegant simplicity of the label. Just below the word Chardonnay it carries the signature of each brother. "One suspects," he says, "that Julio Gallo would have considered it a most appropriate memorial."

He's got that right.

—September 25, 1993

Part VI — Making Connections: Even in this hi-tech world of communications, we still get cut off

Finding a memento

NOW IS THE TIME FOR ALL GOOD people to come to the aid of the county. We are indebted to Ray Simon for the text of today's lesson.

"The county has never given anything to anyone for anything whatsoever," Simon said. It was a Churchillian statement with which many taxpayers would agree. An equal number would probably disagree.

But that's beside the point. As chairman of the Board of Supervisors, Simon was expressing his embarrassment at the county's lack of hospitality toward visiting celebrities and honored guests.

As one example, he cited the recent visit of Walter Cronkite. At the welcoming ceremony, Modesto Mayor Peggy Mensinger graciously presented him with an eight-inch, polished brass, suitably engraved key to the city.

It was a little thing, certainly not an original idea, but television's most celebrated newsman was obviously touched by the gesture even before he noticed that one end of the key is a bottle opener. It would go well on his beloved sailboat, serving both for brass to be polished and beer to be opened.

When it came Simon's turn as the county's highest elected officer to welcome Cronkite, he had nothing tangible to give the most trusted man in America.

He could only smile, hold up his empty hands and say, "Now back to you, Walter."

It makes for an awkward situation, and Simon is right. The county needs to find a fitting memento for its distinguished visitors.

When you think about it, counties generally seem to have been left out of the memento business. Presenting an honored visitor with a key to the city is a gesture of long standing. States are always trying to outdo each other in memorializing the visits of notables. Kentucky makes colonels of them, occasionally even commissioning a Yankee. Nebraska takes them into its navy, bestowing rank up to and including admiral. Heaven only knows what Texas is doing these days.

Finding a suitable token for the county is a special problem, and it's no wonder Simon is asking for help.

Another key is out of the question. Not only is the idea already taken, but nobody ever gives anybody a key to the county. It doesn't even sound right.

In the interest of helping out, we have done some preliminary asking around and can only report that relatively little thought has been given to this subject.

One not very helpful respondent suggested that we give our visitors Newman, but you'll always find one of those in every crowd.

Another said whatever it is, it must include a corkscrew. Maybe a corkscrew in the shape of a dairy cow would be appropriate.

There was a third who suggested that we take a fertile Medfly and mold it into a cube of Lucite. That may be a pregnant idea, but whatever we settle on must be an enduring thing, and we certainly hope the Medfly will soon be gone and forgotten.

Also, we need to remember that our memento must be suitable for either sex. Earrings, for example, would not do because some women don't wear them.

A young person favored something in a T-shirt. She suggested a grassy green with a farm scene and the message: "Yes, Virginia, there is a Stanislaus."

Before you discard that idea, you need to know that almost everybody thought any memento, to be really representative of Stanislaus, had to have some relationship to farming.

We could go back to the key idea and bring it up to date. Instead of a key, we would give them a key-card. That's the plastic card the size of a credit card with a lot of magic and magnetic things on it. You stick in a slot to gain entrance to exclusive clubs,

125

pass through gates of privilege or raise barriers to choice parking places.

On it would be the name of the recipient embossed in gold and with it would come lifetime membership in the Stanislaus County Honor Farm.

With full privileges.

—March 13, 1982

We oughta be in pictures

OUR LIVELY CHAMBER OF COMMERCE is out to make our childhood dreams come true. The chamber wants to put us in the movies.

Having received a few nibbles from promotional mentions in film industry publications, the chamber has decided to launch a more aggressive effort to woo filmmakers to Modesto with the promise of "Timeless beauty ... minutes away."

A handsome color brochure offers a sampling of buildings and scenes of the countryside in a wide circle around Modesto. The scenes are indeed inviting, some of them, in fact, looking like they came right out of a movie. The setting sun nestling into the Coast Range over the grasslands, the well-kept Western look of El Rio Estanislao ranch, a page from the past in a softly sunlit view of the Knights Ferry covered bridge.

The project obviously has the enthusiasm of chamber executive vice president Dave Kilby, who himself contributed some of the color photos for the brochure.

In addition to the pictorial presentation, the brochure assures prospects that the chamber stands ready to provide all possible assistance. Filmmakers are told they will find a community well

126

equipped to furnish all the logistics — housing, catering, transportation, equipment and, if you please, experienced extras.

But don't be misled by Kilby's fervor for his effort. He is not pursuing it like some star-struck kid off the farm. Like any good chamber man, he is looking for "clean economic development."

In his report on the project to the City Council earlier this week, he estimated a movie-making crew could pump $150,000 a week into the local economy. Others think the figure is conservative. Certainly, if we could get Francis Ford Coppola to make something like "Son of Apocalypse" here, we'd all get rich. But his films are so messy. And he takes so long.

There is, of course, a certain risk in all of this. Getting people in here to make films might be one more perilous step toward putting Modesto on the map. Remember, the chamber people are talking not just about films for movie houses. They're talking about television films and even commercials. In no time at all we could be overrun by people with all kinds of over-the-counter medical problems, other wretched souls who have been betrayed by an ephemeral deodorant and a horde of jumpy coffee drinkers pursued by wild-eyed zealots who are out to decaffeinate the world.

Not to worry. The films will not give us away. George Lucas, our own famous filmmaker, taught us that lesson. If you want to make a film about Modesto, you go to Petaluma. If he had made "American Graffiti" in Modesto, nobody would have recognized it. It simply would not have been authentic, unless he wanted to rebuild 10th and 11th streets and restore Burge's Drive-In. Actually, that's not a bad idea, but we'll leave all that up to the Renaissance Committee.

In any case, we hope the chamber has sent a brochure to Lucas. After all, he is quite familiar with the potential around here, and now that he is not making movies about Modesto anymore, he might find that we have just what he needs.

The chamber people make no secret of their aim. They are out to top Stockton in this field. In the 16 years since the Stockton chamber has been actively courting producers, it has provided the setting for 45 movie, television and commercial productions. Single films in 1975 and 1976 alone dumped more that $1 million each into Stockton's economy. The Modesto chamber plans to compete aggressively for a slice of that business.

Good. We're in favor of that. We need to put on the gloves with our friendly neighbors to the north. They're getting a little pushy. They have already swallowed our postmark, they are after our air service and now the telephone company is planning to move our directory service up there.

And all they have ever given us in return is On Lock Sam and Norman Shumway. It's time to go on the offensive.

—April 24, 1982

The driving question

AT LUNCH RECENTLY A YOUNG WOMAN who is a relative newcomer to this area remarked quite negatively on the quality of motor vehicle operators she has encountered here.

In fact, she said in all her experience she has never come across as many lousy drivers per passenger mile as she has in Modesto.

Before going on with this, we need to establish a couple of things. Like, what is a relative newcomer? In some circles that would be almost anybody who is not a middle-aged graduate of Modesto High School. In this case, we mean anybody who has discovered us in the last three to five years.

As for this critic's credentials, she is a child of the mobile generation, well traveled and sufficiently experienced in the challenges of commuting to render reasonable judgments on the comparative skills of her fellow drivers.

In general, she has found Modesto drivers to be inattentive to the demands of driving in traffic. She says they are not aware of the cars around them, and they do not anticipate responses to clearly developing changes in the flow of traffic.

Her most specific criticism is aimed at the number of impulsive lane-changers. No checking the mirrors, no looking around, no using the blinkers. Just a sudden urge to move next door. So far, she says, she has managed to dodge, swerve or brake to avoid these incipient side-swipers, but she is getting apprehensive over the frequency of the occasions.

Now then, how do you like that? We have to admit to some surprise, having never before heard that criticism so broadly applied to this community. That may well result from a preference for walking whenever time or distance allows. And walkers have a different perspective on drivers. We don't trust any of them. We walk defensively. We never challenge them. We even try to avoid letting a driver decide when we can use a crosswalk. We do not wish to flaunt our right-of-way in the snarling face of an impatient driver. And we never, but never, cross the driveway of an alley between buildings without coming to a full stop. Those things are real pedestrian traps.

Categorizing drivers is practiced universally. In France, all drivers enter busy intersections with their eyes closed and horns blowing. In Italy, traffic backs up while two drivers entertain a gathering crowd with an animated, arm-waving argument over who is at fault. In Germany, anybody who does less than 100 mph on the

Autobahn could get run over. In London, they drive on the wrong side of the street, but it's worse in Hong Kong, where they do the same, because all the cars are manned by wild-eyed youngsters who never take time out for tea.

For that matter, in at least 49 other states the favorite epithet for any offending motorist is "California driver." Anyone who has driven in the East knows better. There are exceptions everywhere, of course, but in general Californians, who do a lot of driving, are reasonably considerate. In our experience this is particularly true in the Los Angeles area, where driving is a way of life. L.A. drivers have always seemed especially tolerant of the visitor who invariably finds himself in the wrong lane.

Getting back to the case in point, however, if we are indeed being tagged as a community of lousy drivers, how do we account for it?

Well, we can always blame growth. It has spawned heavier traffic. Scenic Drive is getting like McHenry. Oakdale, Coffee, Briggsmore, Needham, La Loma are all carrying more traffic, and our rush-minute has been extended to five or ten. The traffic on those streets is thicker because we still have so many other streets that don't go anywhere.

And if none of those reasons is satisfactory, we can always blame one other contributing factor: newcomers.

—*June 26, 1982*

Moving right along

GIVE US A LITTLE TIME, PLEASE, TO CATCH our breath. We are having a little trouble keeping up with this go-go City Council.

There is nothing recumbent about these incumbents. They

have more irons in the fire than a cavalry blacksmith.

In what is almost less time than it takes to get across the Briggsmore overpass, they have decided to:

— Go all out to attract new industry.

— Turn the Southern Pacific depot into a transportation center.

— Build their own community center downtown.

— Get the railroad tracks off Ninth Street.

— Slip two underpasses beneath the SP tracks somewhere downtown.

— Remove the Grand Street bottleneck with a new bridge.

— Pipe Tuolumne River water down here before the city's wells give out.

And on the seventh day, they probably will rest, although there may still be some other things demanding their attention — another bridge over the river, for instance, or a left-turn light for Orangeburg Avenue traffic turning into McHenry.

All of these things have been kicking around for a long time. Some of them really never were shelved. It just seems that way.

The sudden burst of energy started with the council's decision to get actively involved in the industry-recruiting business.

The Chamber of Commerce said it was delighted with this new turn of events and would look forward to working closely with the city's new industrial recruiter.

The sudden move last month also to take the initiative in getting started on a downtown community center already has been remarked upon here. It will continue to provoke discussion as the council moves to implement its decision.

In all these years of talking about a community center, however, it is the most positive step taken by the city since the purchase of the old Lincoln School site in 1970.

One of the major drawbacks to the present plan, as we noted, is the continued existence of the railroad tracks on Ninth Street.

Hardly had we remarked on this when the next thing we knew the mayor and half the City Council were back in Washington telling Congressman Tony Coelho that we had to have $15 million to get those tracks away from our community center. That amount will also give us enough for those underpasses.

Underpasses? We haven't heard anything about underpasses since the last time the city reversed the flow of one-way traffic on H Street. That must be at least 20 years ago. Well, why not? We should have had them when the freeway was built.

The other things — the Grand Street bridge and the water plan actually have been in the works for a long time. It will still be a while before we get a new bridge. And it will be even longer before any Tuolumne River water gets piped in here, but the city's getting together with the Modesto Irrigation District for the study is good long-range planning.

All in all, these projects make for a full agenda. They should keep the council pretty well occupied. If not, there are bound to be other things. Sooner or later somebody will discover that the I Street arch is not in conformance with the city sign ordinance.

—March 24, 1984

The Scenic route

BACK IN THE OLDEN DAYS, THEY TELL US, when the high point of the week was to pile everybody into the family car on Sunday afternoon and go for a leisurely ride in the country, Scenic Drive was a very popular route for such an outing.

It was a winding, two-lane road generally following the meandering course of Dry Creek from the edge of the city at Downey Avenue all the way out to Claus Road.

The drive was pleasantly shaded by trees, and once the riders got past the county hospital and the well-kept cemeteries, they were out in the country, winding their way through vineyards and peach orchards. Even then there were some problems with drivers who tried to go too fast, say more than 25 miles an hour, but for the most part the speeders were held down by the frequent sharp curves.

One veteran Scenic watcher dates the downfall of the drive with the widening of the El Vista Bridge in 1972. That was done to accommodate the increasing traffic generated by residential development east of Oakdale Road.

Within a few years the traffic count had doubled, and by 1981 the stretch between the hospital and Sunnyside Drive was carrying 22,000 vehicles a day, giving it the distinction of being the busiest two-lane street in Modesto.

The inevitable work to start widening Scenic started near the end of last July. That seemed rather late in the sunny summer season to get going, but the schedule called for completion in September. The contractors and officials were right about one thing. They said things would really be in a mess during construction, and they were. Traffic was slowed to a crawl and often stopped. It was routed over a pocked and bumpy roadbed as the crews tried to work on one little section of the road at a time. There were some alternate routes, but the problem was that none of them was really handy. They required going out of the way for quite a distance.

The result was that nearly half of those 22,000 vehicles continued to bump and crawl and stall along the torn-up street throughout the summer. September came and Scenic still looked like a disaster area. Work continued on through October, and it wasn't until November when the rains persisted that the contractor gave up, laid down some temporary, patchy pavement on top of the mud and knocked off for the rest of the year.

Work resumed in April, and the widening project finally was completed last month.

In a way, it's odd that Scenic would have so much traffic, because it has never been an easy street to find — especially going out from downtown. Try telling a visitor how to get there some time. You can go out I Street and sneak along Downey to 19th Street and then left to Scenic, or you can take G Street and thread your way back up Burney into a narrow lane behind a paint store marooned on an island and then on to Scenic. Watch out for traffic on your left.

In either case, you must be prepared to brave the Pretzel Parkway that marks the beginning of H Street. It is criss-crossed with little streets running here and there and planted with triangular islands, barricades, traffic lights and even the city's official Christmas tree.

Now the city is embarked on a plan to change all of this. At the moment, however, it looks as if the main purpose is to get cars off Scenic rather than on to it.

Downey Avenue will be reconverted to one-way traffic for its entire length, meaning you will no longer be able to find Scenic from I Street. The only access will be the G Street roundabout to Burney, which will also be one-way from that intersection to its junction with Scenic behind the paint store.

Nobody has mentioned the main problem. The main problem

is H Street. It actually provided the most direct access to Scenic Drive — runs right into it with no loop-the-loops, just as J Street runs into McHenry. The only difficulty is that H Street is a one-way street going the wrong-way. It would be much too expensive to change it back again, and besides, we've already done that once.

Maybe the plan will help Scenic by discouraging traffic. If that works, perhaps next we can try hiding La Loma.

—June 8, 1985

Keeping in touch

OUR FRIENDS FROM THE BAY AREA called to check in and see how things were going. They knew how things were going. They just wanted another opportunity to make their snide little remarks and show off their big-city airs.

First, they wanted to commiserate on the failure of the library tax measure. They said they understood that the libraries would be open only every other Wednesday, the bookmobile has mothballed, the children's story hour has been dropped, the reference desk has been closed and the remaining staff has been instructed not to smile anymore.

Well, that's not exactly what happened, but close enough to the truth to hurt. They couldn't understand how this could be. They mentioned that San Francisco is only now getting ready to enlarge its library facilities with a big new building in the civic center.

We reminded them that there could hardly be any comparison. In the first place, San Francisco is both a city and county, which eliminates a certain amount of buck-passing, turf battling and tax revenue sharing. Moreover the city is now starting to get rich from the power it generates with our Tuolumne River water and has

135

always done a pretty good business with parking tickets, tow-away fees, hotel taxes and other forms of tourist-gouging.

They also complained about traffic, and we offered sympathy but reminded that this is just one of the joys of living in a major metropolitan area. They weren't talking about Bay Area traffic, they said. They can handle that. It's increased traffic on the way to Modesto.

They find it is fairly smooth until they come out of Niles Canyon into San Ramon and Livermore. Then all these automobiles come pouring out of these big new office parking lots and start heading for Tracy and Manteca.

It's getting to the place that the Altamont Pass now has more cars than windmills. Why are all these people heading to Tracy and Manteca?

Several reasons. First of all, they live there. A good many of them got priced out of the Bay Area, the same as the buildings did. Another reason is that either of those places is easier to find than Modesto, although there has been some spillover and we may be losing ground in that respect.

Our friends said they now make it a point to bypass the Manteca bypass. What they do is follow the Los Angeles signs and then turn off on Highway 132. They think they go through Vernalis, although they don't recall ever having seen Vernalis.

Can't blame them for taking that route. Manteca worked long and hard to get that bypass, and now the city is growing out to it. Not only that, when Caltrans finally did get around to building it, they pleaded poverty and built a highway designed for instant obsolescence. It's a two, and occasionally three, lane undivided highway that will have Manteca looking for a by-bypass before the decade is out.

Our friends were not very complimentary about Modesto traffic, either. They said they were baffled by the various speed limits. They couldn't find any pattern. A wide street like College is posted for 25 mph, while a narrow, congested street like Morris has a 35 mph limit, for instance. The limits vary from 25 to 45 as you go along for reasons that are not apparent.

We explained to them that we use the state system of set-it-yourself speed limits. We clock the traffic to see how fast most of the drivers are going and then set the limit at that speed.

What our friends really called for, however, was to get in on a couple of contests. They had heard that Intracity Transit is offering prizes for naming a bus, and the city is looking for a name for the community center.

We told them they were a little late for the bus contest. It ends today. Their offerings were not very inspired, anyway. They suggested Out of Service, Wayward, Desire, Exact Change, Running Late, Old Smokey, Omni and Blunder. Their favorite name was Anonybus.

They were a little cagier about their ideas for the community center, since the contest still has a few days to go.

They did toss off a few obvious ones. Center of Controversy, Grant's Pass, El Centro Modesto and Perseverance Plaza.

They said they did consider trying to work in the Gallo name, but decided against it.

Afraid of being sued.

—September 6, 1986

Polishing the image

WELL, IN SPITE OF EVERYTHING WE'VE done, it looks as though we're losing the battle. We've restricted access from the freeway. We've held down signs pointing to Modesto. We moved Amtrak out to Riverbank. We had our postmark changed. We even lengthened the trains on Ninth Street. It isn't working. People know about us.

The Modesto Chamber of Commerce just completed their Modesto Image Project, and the findings are most revealing.

To get the outsiders' view the survey team compiled a list of 202 Bay Area business firms and set out to contact the chief executive of each one. They managed to get responses from 139 and of that number only two (2) said they had never heard of Modesto.

We had always supposed that the number would be much greater than that. But we suspect this is the direct result of the commuter invasion from the Bay Area. The word is getting around, and we are getting the spillover from Tracy and Manteca.

Of the remaining 137 executives, 118 said they had been to or through Modesto. And that's about all. More than half of these said they had absolutely no idea of what Modesto is all about. Most of them had just passed through from time to time.

So, we are left with 63 Bay Area business executives who said they were either somewhat aware or well aware of our community, and it is with them we are concerned.

Asked for their overall perception of Modesto, nearly a third of them said small town. The tactful ones said things like nice place, farming, growing. Three blunt ones said hick town, and seven said hot.

But the small town and hick town perceptions, even though

they are not quite synonymous, can be explained by the executives' estimate of our population. Some 15 of them thought we were still less than 50,000, 18 put us at between 50,000 and 100,000, and 17 were closer to the mark at 100,000 to 200,000. But 7 of them estimated us at more than 200,000. They must have passed through by way of McHenry Avenue on Graffiti Night.

We can understand why so many executives' acquaintance with Modesto is limited to "passing through." They might stop and look around a little if they knew how to get off the freeway.

Anybody who has tried to direct a visitor on how to get off the freeway and where to go after that can sympathize with them.

We recently had a Bay Area executive call and ask directions for driving to Modesto and specifically for getting to the Holiday Inn.

We told him to take 580 through the Altamont, then 205 behind Tracy into I-5 and on to 120 around Manteca and into 99.

He said he was reasonably familiar with all that. What he needed to know was which exit to take when he got to Modesto.

There was this long pause, until he finally said well, do you know or don't you know.

We said yes, we knew, and we wished him luck. We took a deep breath and told him to take the Briggsmore-Carpenter exit, go to the top of the overpass, turn left at the light, go to the bottom of the overpass and turn left at the light. Go past the gas stations and around the curve and there you are.

We fixed him. He will never ask us for directions again. He claimed he did exactly what we told him. He took the Briggsmore overpass, turned left at the light, turned left again at the next light and found himself back on the freeway headed for Sacramento.

He had to go all the way to the Salida mall before he could get back on the freeway, and when he got to Briggsmore this time, he couldn't get on the exit because cars were backed up on it right out to the freeway.

So, he kept on going and decided to take the Highway 132 off-ramp. He turned left on 132, crossed the tracks and ran smack into a one-way street going the wrong way. Finally, no longer trusting us, he phoned the people he was going to meet at the Holiday Inn, and they came and escorted him back.

Some of our defenses are still working.

—August 15, 1987

Too good to last

WELL, THE HANDWRITING IS ON the wall. Modesto is on the verge of doing away with — or at least changing — the greatest, the most useful and convenient public service any city could render.

The City Council won't decide for a few months yet, but it is pretty obvious that members are leaning toward combining garden refuse pickup with garbage service by going to the 90-gallon can. This means, of course, that lawn and garden pickup will no longer be free. Nor will it be easy. Or, at any rate, not nearly as convenient as it is now.

Free and easy. That's what has always made the present service so great. It is one of the few things the city does for us throughout the year with virtually no strings attached. We don't have to have a license. We aren't limited only to special days when we can put the stuff out, and even the quantity — which can get pretty sizable at certain times of the year — never seems to daunt the city pickup crews. They just come along with their big mechanical claw, scoop up the stuff and haul it off.

140

Our friends in outlying areas who have never enjoyed such painless service have always looked on with ill concealed envy, occasionally clucking about how spoiled we were. We had only to see what they routinely go through in disposing of garden refuse to realize they are probably right.

They bag up all their lawn cuttings in big plastic bags and cut up all their tree trimmings in little pieces and bag them or put them in boxes. Then, when it's convenient — which it never is — they pile the stuff in the back of the car and haul it off somewhere — probably to a dumpster of their acquaintance, if they are lucky enough to know someone who will let them use it.

The days of continued free garden refuse pickup actually were numbered from the moment the city and its planners decided that residential subdivisions could be developed without alleys. They were under pressure by developers to adopt this policy because it meant the builders could get an extra lot or two out of the subdivisions.

But it was a major mistake, in our opinion, even a worse mistake than in the relatively short period of time when the city also caved in to developers and allowed them to put in subdivisions without sidewalks.

The sidewalk lapse could be rectified — and has been for the most part. The city eventually reinstated the sidewalk requirement and began helping unhappy homeowners in the walkless subdivisions to put in their own a block at a time.

But the cost of remedying the alley deficiency is now prohibitive. And it's a shame. Because alleys are a very useful part of our urban infrastructure. They provide an ideal place to run out water, sewer and gas lines as well as the underground power and telephone lines that now serve the newer areas.

141

They offer quick and easy access for construction and repair equipment whenever there is any trouble and save digging up a street and blocking traffic.

Alleys are also a good place to meet and talk with neighbors — even those across the way who live one street over. They help to extend the neighborhood.

But the really great thing about alleys is that they are a perfect place to put lawn and garden trimmings. And it is the absence of alleys in the newer sections of the city that has added strength to the city's argument for a change in the service. Residents of the alley-less areas have no alternative but to dump their trimmings in the street, which not only blocks off curb space but makes for increasingly unsightly streets.

The city also says the absence of grass clippings in the streets will improve storm drainage, particularly in areas served by dry wells.

We once lived in an area that had both alleys and dry wells, however, and we wouldn't look for any great improvement in storm drainage. Dry wells without grass clippings work all right if you give them about a week in between heavy rains to drain off a flooded street.

In any case, be prepared to bid farewell to a truly useful and convenient service.

Then sit back and await the next blessing of progress.

—April 16, 1988

Where there's Hope...

BOB HOPE IS INDISPUTABLY THE DEAN of America's stand-up comedians. His greatest fame comes from having entertained our troops in three wars and various other police actions, taking his entire troupe right out to the troops in the war zone. Hope, who will celebrate his 85th birthday in May, rejects any thought of retiring and seems to be in a race for longevity with George Burns, who marked his 92nd birthday earlier this year.

Actually, Hope is a very thorough and methodical comedian. He has a file of jokes and gags and one-liners that would tax the storage capacity of a main frame computer. It is one of the keys to his success.

The other one is that Hope always insists that his material be tailored to his audience. So we can expect some local material to be inserted into his show when he appears here next Saturday for the opening of the Modesto Centre Plaza.

As it happens, we have come into possession of a draft script for Saturday's Hope show here from a source we are not at liberty to divulge. We can't vouch for the authenticity of this material, but we thought we would share it anyway for the benefit of those of us who will be unable to attend:

EMCEE: And now, ladies and gentlemen, the event you have all been waiting for, it is my privilege and pleasure to introduce America's ambassador of comedy, Mr. Bob Hope.

(Theme up. Hope strides onto stage smiling and wide-eyed to thunderous applause)

HOPE: Thank you, ladies and gentlemen. Thank you. Thank you very much. I want to thank Mayor Whiteside and the members of Omega Nu for this opportunity. It is really great to be in . . .

Modesto. This is my first time here. And it won't be my last. I promised Mike Herrero I would come back when Allen Grant opens the Red Lion Hotel. Mike said I would be older than George Burns by then.

When the Omega Nu people invited me here, I asked them to tell me a little bit about this center and how it came into being. Afterwards, I said sure I'd come. I've spent most of my career entertaining fighting men and women wherever they are.

The mayor was a little concerned about our finding Modesto. We had no problems. We knew we were here when we spotted the Gallos. Julio was out in the yard making a batch of Hearty Burgundy and Ernest was up at the front gate telling Joe he couldn't come in. He told Joe to leave his name and he'd get back to him,

We didn't see anything of Bartles and Jaymes. This was their day to go out and pick berries.

The city sent a car out to the airport for us. On the way in, the driver told us about Mr. Ralston and how Modesto got its name. I could dig that. My good friend Tony Coelho once wanted to put a bill in to have my face carved into Mt. Rushmore, but I declined out of modesty. I did ask the president what he thought of the idea. He said he'd sign the bill but he'd have to ask Nancy about it. Nancy just said no. How about that Nancy? Isn't she something? She thought it was too dangerous. She was afraid they would try to turn the nose into a ski jump.

We pulled into the new parking garage and took the footbridge over here. Good thing we did. There was a train coming down the street. That footbridge is nice, but there's something I want to tell you. Watch out for that last step!

Rich Singer told me there had been some last-minute problems with access, but he wanted to assure me that the building provided full access for everyone. He took me all around. He even showed me a door out back next to the service entrance. It was marked reserved for Richard Patterson and Pat McGrath.

And I think it's nice the way all the rooms in this building have names. Just before coming on I visited the Bob Oliver Men's Room. It's very nice. It's just down the hall out there. You can't miss it. It's right next to the Zagaris Brothers Broom Closet.

And now, ladies and gentlemen, I want to thank you for your hospitality. You've been a great audience, and I'll see you at the Red Lion. Yessir.

> *(Theme up)*
> HOPE (singing)
>> *Thanks for the memories*
>> *Of Modesto and its trees*
>> *Of bibliophiles and tire piles*
>> *And Joseph Gallo's cheese*
>> *We thank you so much.*
>> *Many's the time we've tried*
>> *Briggsmore*
>> *And many's the time we*
>> *cruised 'Henry*
>> *Oh well, it's great to have Centree*
>> *We did have funds and*
>> *overruns*
>> *So thank you, so much.*
>
> *—March 5, 1988*

Part VII — English Spoken Here: Nurturing the Mother Tongue

Abusing the language

IN THE COURSE OF PICKING AND PACKAGING the news of the day, most newspaper editors come to think of themselves as guardians of the written language. Or if they don't, they should. They work with it all day long, sharpening it here, polishing it there and correcting it always. Language is their product, and when it leaves their shop it should be in good shape.

Good copy editors take pride in tightening up a story. They get fussy about words. They throw out unnecessary ones, they replace fuzzy ones with precise ones and they absolutely do not tolerate abused ones.

How come, then, that American newspapers are coming under more and more criticism for misuse of the language? The bad marks are coming not only from the purists in academia but from sensitive readers. And their concerns are not just addressed to accurate and concise usage, but to the basics of grammar, spelling and syntax.

Faced with horrible examples from their own daily product, responsible editors are shaking their heads in public and shaking up their newsrooms in private. They may be mystified about what happened to a discipline that once seemed securely built-in, but they are more concerned about reinstating it. The emphasis has always been, and remains, to get the story and get it right. Now, emphasis on care and precision in writing is getting more attention than ever.

One of the early editorial guardians of the language was the late Ted Bernstein of the *New York Times*. He pioneered a critique with his in-house publication of "Winners and Sinners," giving examples of good and bad usage culled daily from the *Times*. His work is still carried on by Allan Siegal.

In the course of his work, Bernstein published several books on the use of language. In one of them, "The Careful Writer," he had something to say about the influences that were adversely affecting the written language.

One of them, he said, was the confusion over the difference between the spoken language and the written language. He had no patience with the school of thought that says spoken language is the language, that usage determines what is acceptable and that we must abandon ideas of right and wrong, good and bad, correct and incorrect. "The language of today," these linguists say, "is not to be identified with that found in books but is to be found chiefly on the lips of people who are currently speaking it."

Bernstein would have none of it. "Let us not hesitate to assert," he asserts, "that 'The pencil was laying on the table' and 'He don't know nothing' are at present incorrect no matter how many know-nothings say them. Let us insist that disinterested be differentiated from uninterested, not as a fetish but as a means of preserving a word that is needful...Let us do these things not to satisfy 'rules' or to gratify the whims of a pedagogue, but rather to express ourselves clearly, precisely and directly..."

David Shaw, the *Los Angeles Times* media critic, recently explored the rising outcry over the abuse of the language in print.

He found that most editors and critics believe that what we are now experiencing is the direct result of academic permissiveness in the '60s. There is general agreement that the do-your-own-thing era contributed significantly to the deterioration of language instruction and usage.

The erosion in literacy is laid in large measure to the relaxation of reading assignments coupled with greater reliance on television for information and entertainment.

One critic claims the decline started much earlier than the '60s. She thinks it began with the de-emphasis on the study of foreign languages, particularly the abandonment of Latin. She notes, as an example, that because she studied Latin she could not possibly misspell the word *accommodate*. Few people today can face that word with such confidence. Yet, certainly, today's greater reliance on spoken language, in which spelling is not a factor, has done the most to disfigure the written language.

The remedial effort could begin quite modestly. It would be nice to stop seeing such things as *their's* and *publically* and *accidently*. *Accommodate* is a tall order. It's a lot like *Mississippi* — and the fourth grader who said he knew how to spell it; he just didn't know when to stop.

—*May 9, 1981*

The state of things

JANUARY IS THE MONTH FOR TAKING STOCK. Maybe it is a custom that spilled over from the mercantile field.

It's the inventory period — time for counting up what's on hand to get a picture of how things went last year and make plans for the year ahead.

As a result we get a lot of summary messages. We find out about the state of the union, the state of the state, the state of the art and even about the state of the city. (For some reason, we don't hear much about the state of the county, but we always find out about it around election time.)

Modesto's Mayor Peggy Mensinger broke with tradition this year and delivered her state of the city speech first to Network, a women's organization. She previously has followed the custom of her predecessor, former Mayor Lee Davies, in making the annual address before the Rotary Club. She didn't skip Rotary, you understand. She just went to Network first.

The chivalrous Rotarians didn't seem to mind, and there was no way they could fine her for being late.

Of all the messages floating around this year, we haven't seen one on the state of the language, even though one is surely long overdue.

The longstanding campaign of former U.S. Senator S. I. "Sam" Hayakawa to establish English as the nation's official language is still going on.

Last November, Californians voted heavily in favor of Proposition 38, a ballot measure requiring the governor to urge the federal government to get rid of the bilingual ballot.

Now Hayakawa is lending his support to a proposal by a Southern California assemblyman to have English declared the official language of California.

Before we fully embrace English to the exclusion of all other languages, however, we need to get busy and learn it. Particularly in its written form. It's slowly slipping away from us.

Take the lowly apostrophe, for example. It is gradually disappearing or showing up in the wrong place. Maybe it's because the apostrophe is an overworked symbol. It is the sign of the possessive. It denotes a contraction, and it is also used to designate a quotation within a quotation.

Perhaps our road and directional signs have something to do with this. Words are rapidly being replaced by symbols. "Slippery when wet" is replaced by a little car with squiggly lines behind it. "Deer Xing" gives way to a fawn prancing across a yellow signboard. And every kind of no-no is pictured in a circle with a red line drawn through it. Even the pedestrian walk-wait signals are being replaced by upraised hands and walking men.

We aren't sure whether all these things reflect a growing cosmopolitanism or increasing illiteracy. We also wonder what the effect this legal emphasis on English would have on linguistically lazy Americans who already expect everybody everywhere to speak English.

It is a coincidence that a member of Hayakawa's ancestral homeland recently commented on tongue-tied Americans. In an article in the Japanese newspaper *Sankei Shimbun*, a Tokyo professor of international relations says the increased trade and business connections between the two nations have made little difference. Very few Americans, even those who live in Japan, make any attempt to learn the language.

The professor, who considers himself pro-American, says he can live with that, but not with the failure of Americans to inform themselves of the customs of the countries they visit.

As an example, he notes that on President Reagan's visit to Tokyo, the president crossed his legs during a televised press conference with Japanese reporters, and crossing one's legs in public is not considered good manners in Japan.

It is the first time we've heard of the president being criticized on that count. For crossing his heart or maybe his fingers, yes, but never for crossing his legs.

—*January 12, 1985*

The official language

WHEN THE NEWS REACHED THE MOTHER Country, the Keeper of the Queen's English said he was positively enthralled by the renaissance in the Colonies, particularly the one called California.

After all these years, he said, who would have dreamt that those lost sheep who had strayed so far from the fold would return to declare English their official language. It will jolly well take some doing, he agreed, but the overwhelming vote by which the masses demonstrated their favour for this proposition shows it to be a labour of love.

The Keeper said he would be looking for evidence of progress soon in all our printed outpourings, but hoped we also would give some attention to the pronunciation of such words as laboratory, schedule and tuppence, although it was not Her Majesty's wish that anyone go to gaol over any breach of speech.

Heaven knows we are most anxious to do our part right here in downtown Modesto. We have already named our future civic gathering place the Modesto Centre Plaza. Granted, that is only one for three, it will take some time before we can think of converting it to Modest Center Place.

After all, as the mayor pointed out, we do have some other elements to consider in our heritage, including a Spanish land grant and a Mexican railroad worker who was trying to make points with the big boss. Also, the word plaza has come into the English language, having once been favoured by swanky hotels and currently enjoying considerable popularity among shopping centers and tolltakers' booths.

In any case, it probably doesn't matter what official name we give the centre, it very likely will take on a name of its own after it's up and running. We can only hope it will inspire an endearing one, but at this point, who knows? We always thought Modesto Metropolitan Square would serve nicely, knowing that it would inevitably be shortened to Metro Square, and that's even better. That may sound presumptuous at this time, but it won't by the end of the century. That's another idea. We could call it Modesto New Century Square. Too late. The contest is over.

The effects of the passage of Proposition 63, declaring English to be California's official language, are not over, however. They are just beginning. At first, we figured some of the claims about what would happen were overblown, but now we're not so sure. Never underestimate the reach of a zealot. Some of these people care very much about converting everything to English.

What all this most likely will amount to is a full employment program for lawyers. And speaking of lawyers, what does this new initiative mean for them? Will they have to start practicing law in English? Will they have to make do without all the *ipsos* and *factos*, forsake the *prima facie* cases and give up the *quid pro quos*?

And then there are doctors. They also use a lot of Latin. Even the *Rx* symbol for prescription comes from the Latin word for *recipe*. Will they no longer be able to write in Latin: Take two aspirin and call me manana?

In either case, it probably doesn't matter. Hardly anybody can read a doctor's handwriting in any language. And even when said lawyers speak in said English, only other lawyers can understand them.

There probably is no point in getting all worked up over these things, anyway. Governing bodies, we have learned over the years, find imaginative ways of dealing with problems created by their predecessors. This week, the Turlock City Council gave us a lesson in handling blight.

Back when there were no sign regulations, this furniture store which was then on the outskirts of Turlock, erected a towering 104-foot, two-legged sign, thrusting a latticework of neon into the sky that was easily visible on a clear night from downtown Keyes, five miles away.

When Turlock decided to put limits on signs about 10 years ago, the existing ones were grandfathered in with the usual provision that whenever there was a change — either in the sign or the ownership — the sign would have to be made to conform with current regulations.

When the owner wanted to make a slight change in the sign, he was initially told he would have to scale the whole thing down to size. He didn't want to do that. He reminded city officials that the sign had been in place for 40 years.

And that gave them the answer. They designated the sign an historic landmark, which means it will stand forevermore — or at least until the council's successors figure out a way of undoing this one.

We're not sure a 40-year-old sign deserves historic status, but certainly the Turlock council's action is a landmark decision.

Enough of this. It's time for a spot of tea.

—November 15, 1986

Now, a few words...

ONE THING WE HAVE ALWAYS BEEN grateful to the English language for is its simplicity, its flexibility and its adaptability.

The old saying is that the Greeks had a word for it, and we're sure they did because we have borrowed a lot of them.

That's part of the genius of English. Whenever we need a word to fit a new thing or a new situation, we'll find it somewhere — whether it's from another language or from off the streets or just a new meaning for an existing word.

If the word comes from another language, we might acknowledge that for a while by trying to use its native pronunciation, but if the word really fits and comes into wide usage, we'll take it into our language and frequently give it our own pronunciation. Sometimes we'll even shorten it a little.

Take the French word for overthrow of the government, coup d'etat. We seem to prefer that expression to our own probably because we have dropped half of it and just use the word coup.

We suspect headline writers had a lot to do with that usage, but now we have taken the word into our language to mean any upset, brilliant stroke or general housecleaning. And we suspect the sports writers had something to do with that.

The French, on the other hand, strongly resist that kind of mongrelization of their own language. They have an academy that does nothing but watch over the language in an effort to keep it pure.

It's not altogether a winning battle, however, largely because the American teen culture of music and clothes and fast food has a universal way of creeping in — much to the continuing dismay of the French purists. That's all right. We have a debt to anybody who gave us hors d'oeuvres — such an unappetizing word for appetizers.

English also has a neat way of shortening a pretentious word to get right to the point. No one has to say, "If you have a facsimile machine, we will send it to you by facsimile." Rather, they just say, "If you have a fax, we'll fax it to you." A nice little three-letter word serving as both noun and verb. Fax isn't in the dictionary yet, but there's no doubt it will be.

Another example of English simplicity is the formation of the plural. For the most part, all we have to do is add an "s" or "es" to the noun and we've got it.

Not so in many other languages. To form the plural, the noun has to change, any adjective modifying it has to change and the article has to change. La casa grande becomes las casas grandes. The Germans don't even use the "s" for plurals. They use an "e" or an "n" or an "en" or nothing at all, according to rules that only a German understands, but the articles and adjectives have to change, too.

English does have some exceptions, like mouse and mice, tooth and teeth, mostly to accommodate the spoken word. Mouses and tooths just don't sound right.

And sometimes we get into trouble with words of Greek and Latin derivation. One we hear frequently these days is honoraria as the plural of honorarium. It just hasn't been around long enough. Look what happened to memorandum. It went from memoranda to memorandums to memos.

Then we have these funny plurals that are most often, even if incorrectly, used in the singular, like data and media. Data is the plural of datum, but we hardly ever see a datum anymore. What we see is data by the megabyte.

Media refers to the various means of mass communication — radio, television, newspapers, magazines and maybe even motion pictures. We see it used so often in the singular that it now has a plural of its own — medias.

Media started out as the plural of medium, although mediums is a perfectly acceptable plural. We don't use the word medium in this sense much anymore, probably because of its association with the occult.

In other words, it's too spooky.

—*March 25, 1989*

Language lesson

A WHILE BACK, WE NOTED THE APOSTROPHE was on its way to disappearing from the English language — mainly, it seems, because nobody knows how to use it.

The biggest stumbler for a lot of people is *its* vs. *it's*, and that's largely because the apostrophe serves two separate functions. One is to denote a possessive and the other is to indicate a contraction.

It's time for the dog to have its bath.

Confusion is compounded by the fact that the apostrophe is never used for possessive pronouns — *his, hers, ours, yours, its.*

Another point of confusion comes with plural nouns. An apostrophe is never used in a simple plural. A card from the Smith family is signed *The Smiths*. It is used to denote a possessive when we say it's time for the Smiths' dog to have its bath.

Now we understand there is a movement under way to eliminate the apostrophe. The simple solution. Since nobody knows how to use it, get rid of it. Well, we object.

Who could be behind such a movement and who is in a position to make and carry out such a decision?

The National Association of English Teachers and the publishers of dictionaries have a great deal of influence over language usage, as well they should. But it's doubtful either one of them would have anything to do with abolition of the apostrophe.

What we fear may have more influence over present-day usage than any other single group is advertising. Admen are ready to sacrifice any rule of grammar if they can come up with what they believe is a catchy phrase. *Winston tastes good like a cigarette should* or *you got the right one, baaaby. Uh-huh.*

Other abuses frequently creep into television, not just from men and women on the street or from game show participants, but from hosts and emcees and other pros whose business is language and who should know better.

Such as, *Just between you and I*. And, *it is the hope of my wife and I*, etc.

It's remarkable the role the ear plays in the acceptance of usage, particularly with *I* vs. *me*. Who but a poet would say, *It is I*, instead of *It's me*.

And who but a stuffy grammarian would insist on, *It's I, It's I, It's I, oh Lord?* Or *I and my shadow?*

Speaking of plain language, we were fortunate to catch former Sen. Barry Goldwater on Jay Leno's *Tonight Show* this week, and the old guy (he's 85 now) is just as alert and peppery as ever.

It's been almost 30 years since Goldwater ran against Lyndon Johnson for the presidency and was widely hailed as Mr. Conservative.

Compared with today's breed of conservatives, Goldwater comes through as a thoughtful, plain-speaking moderate.

In fact, when we thought about all the candidates in the recent election who tried to evoke the image of Harry Truman, we were struck by the thought that Goldwater, in his outlook, his philosophy, his style, has more in common with Truman than any of them.

Asked about gays in the military, he said he had been in and out of the service for about 50 years and never in all that time had he ever had any officer, any general bring up any problem in connection with homosexual activity. What's all the fuss?

He was on the night that Vice President Al Gore and Ross Perot debated the North American Free Trade Agreement. Leno asked him about NAFTA, and Goldwater said Arizona had always profited from excellent relations with Mexico.

"And if it works for Arizona," he said, "it ought to work for the whole country."

Leno asked him about Perot. Did he think Perot would make a good president?

"Well," Goldwater said, "if I had some question about business, I'd go to Perot. If I were looking for someone to run the nation, I wouldn't.

You wouldn't be in favor of him for president? Leno asked.

"Not of this country," Goldwater answered flatly.

He was at his most candid when Leno asked him about former President Richard Nixon.

Goldwater said in the middle of Watergate when he found out what had really happened he went to Nixon and told him he should lay it all out and apologize to the people. He said Nixon agreed that was a good idea and he'd do it.

"But he didn't," Goldwater said. "He just went on lying. He lied to his wife, to his children, to his supporters, to the people."

Asked if he had seen Nixon since he resigned, Goldwater said just once. "And that was one time too many."

Now that's plain language. But not very conservative.

—November 13, 1993